Finding God

ONE PSYCHOLOGIST'S JOURNEY

Dennis Alne Ph.D.

BALBOA
PRESS

A DIVISION OF HAY HOUSE

Balboa Press books may be ordered through booksellers or by contacting:

Balboa Press
A Division of Hay House
1663 Liberty Drive
Bloomington, IN 47403
www.balboapress.com
1 (877) 407-4847

Print information available on the last page.

ISBN: 978-1-5043-5788-3 (sc)
ISBN: 978-1-5043-5789-0 (e)

Balboa Press rev. date: 03/10/2017

CONTENTS

Acknowledgements xi
Introduction.. xiii

The Early Years...1
Troubled Teens 9
Crisis 1 12
My Downfall 17
My Awakening...22
Best decision I ever made...26
Crisis Two 32
Disability...34
Treating patients with disabilities 39
Training in Psychopharmacology 46
Crisis 3 51
The Growth of Science 54
Cosmological Surprises..63
Scientific Research Speeds Up 70
Entanglement, Nonlocality and Holography 73
Biology chimes in 79
Paranormal Behaviors..85
Paranormal Research Becomes Respected 95
Medium Research 100
Near Death and Out Of Body Experiences 104
Speculations on Brain Functioning.. 116
Reincarnation 118
Implications for Healthcare..120

Prayer and the Sick..128
The Power of Faith 131
Compassion and Healthcare..134
I'm a New Man...136
Integrating Spirituality into Psychotherapy 137
Healthcare Recommendations...147
Wisdom of Our Ancestors 152
Science can initiate the Revival 157

Conclusion..161
Appendix 1..167
References...171

A passionate reflection on the journey of a truly dedicated psychologist, determined to "make a difference" in the lives of his fellow citizens.

Pat DeLeon,
former American Psychological Association President

This book is dedicated to my wife. For thirty- six years you have been by my side offering your support and guidance. I will always love you.

ACKNOWLEDGEMENTS

During the preparation of this book I was greatly benefitted by advice. No man is an island. Bruce Kerievsky, for years, was the editor for the newsletter of the Association for Spirituality and Psychotherapy. Bruce graciously offered to edit my manuscript. I added additional content following his edits so any errors are mine. My wife and daughters reviewed the manuscript and offered advice and encouragement. My daughter Maria gets a special nod for helping her tech challenged dad. Finally a number of friends, with different areas of expertise, reviewed the manuscript. Their comments were insightful and proved helpful. Thank you all.

INTRODUCTION

All books have a goal in mind and I have mine. Actually I have a few goals. After thirty-four years of practicing as a clinical psychologist I have learned much about human behavior and helped maybe two thousand patients. I semi-retired in September of 2013, and now that I had the time began to review my life and decided to share my insights with a wider audience.

I know that I sometimes learn best by being shown how to accomplish something. Therefore I decided to use myself as an example of how to overcome life crises. The book you are about to read will allow you to follow me on a journey, through trials and tribulations, to personal growth and deep happiness. Along the way you will learn how best to overcome drug and alcohol addictions, lose the fear of panic attacks, and cope with life altering changes. The final crisis I personally overcame led me to a world that had never been a part of my life before. I am talking about the new scientific paradigm and spirituality.

My hope is that I will make the point to never give up, but keep learning and keep growing as a person. A famous man, one we all know, once said "He who lives in the past will stay in the past." Living life in the present opens up new vistas and offers the possibility for personal growth. Holding on to anger, past injustices, or feeling sorry for one's self, is a ball and chain that will stunt attempts at personal growth. If *Finding God* can help even a few people avoid this mistake I will count it a gain.

The book will be divided into sections. In the first section I will begin with the early years; then move on to the troubled teens and the first crisis in my life. I will next show how in my mid twenties personal insight literally saved my life and started me on a path towards personal growth. This will be followed by the years of clinical practice and child rearing. I will describe my years working as a crisis psychologist for the Brooklyn High Schools and the incident that left me disabled and brought on the second crisis in my life. I observed so many people's lives destroyed due to disability, including my mother's, that I will spend time describing how best to overcome it. I will end with the third crisis, which led me to the path that took me deeply into science and spirituality. Yes, science led me to believe deeply in God. This final crisis allowed me to learn absolutely amazing things. I guarantee that the final section will literally blow your mind as it has mine. The world changed drastically when we broke the atom and found out that the energy particles that make it up obey none of the laws of physics we had believed in for three hundred years.

It is my personal wish that this book will help those who are struggling with past injustices to move beyond them and those who have suffered disabling injuries to realize that there is hope and it comes mostly from inside one's self. Finally, to help all to come to see that the new paradigm of physics which began when the atom was broken and Pandora's box was opened has changed the world that we thought we knew. Regarding this last, if fundamental particles of matter, particles that have little or no mass, can be in multiple places at the same time, can somehow communicate with each other across the galaxy and in a timeless fashion, can change their very reality from a wave to a point particle when they are being observed, and can alter behavior that has already occurred, we must rethink what we thought was reality. A new world has been opened up to us. No longer can the paranormal be so easily dismissed and neither can the power of prayer. Never, in my lifetime, did I expect to see scientifically designed research studies supporting the survival of consciousness after death. The final chapters will explore these. My many colleagues who are atheists because they believe science has debunked God and religions will be shown how wrong they are.

Come with me on this journey and I assure you that your mind will be open to new and exciting possibilities that will lead to your own personal enrichment and happiness.

THE EARLY YEARS

I was born September 10th, 1947. My brother Richard and sister Lorraine are ten and eleven years older than me. Once my mother did tell me that they had planned on stopping at two children, but then my parents had too much to drink at a New Year's Eve party and lo and behold nine months later they received a gift. I am so thankful that abortion was unlawful in those days. Not that my mother would have had one, but just in case. The nurses had nicknamed me "squeaky" since I had my first asthma attack in the hospital nursery. Asthma hounded me throughout my childhood, and there were no medicines for it back in the late 1940's and early 1950's. I once figured out that I had missed around twenty days of school each year in elementary school due to asthma. Struggling to breathe is a horror that I wouldn't wish on anyone. My parents were both heavy smokers and the walls of our house were yellow from smoke. I will always remember lying in bed for weeks gasping for air and having only my teddy bear for comfort. I learned to play a game. I would cover my head and my teddy and I would make believe we were having a party with ice cream and cake. Imagination, for children, is such a useful tool in coping. There is one instance that I will always remember. While I cannot remember all details of my illness I do remember that I was running a high fever. All of a sudden as I was in a dream like state, which I now think of as a lucid dream state, I felt my head growing larger and then suddenly I was floating up to the ceiling and looking down on my body. What was amazing was that at this time I felt absolutely no pain or discomfort. It was as if I was free of all earthly burdens. The feeling was pure peace and comfort. This memory has stayed with me always, and today with what I have learned has a deeper meaning to me. When I reached my teen years and rarely was in the house my asthma improved. Today it hardly bothers me. I rarely use my asthma inhaler when it does. A full glass of water usually helps. I read that in a book about hydration and asthma.

I grew up in a most wonderful place. Gerritsen Beach was a little known fishing enclave in Southern Brooklyn. It was almost like living in the country. There was but one avenue leading into it, and the same avenue leading out. Up until hurricane Sandy almost no one ever heard of it. As you came into the beach the left side of Gerritsen Avenue was open grassland ending in tall weeds and finally an inlet of Jamaica Bay. As a child my friends and I spent hours searching the weeds for frogs and chasing rabbits. We also played hide and seek in the weeds. There were so many children to play with. We were the baby boom generation. Every summer the Gerritsen Beach Association would devote one day to orphans. Buses would bring a large number of children from orphanages. The fishing fleet would take the children fishing in the morning. A huge barbecue would follow this with games in the afternoon. Many people from Gerritsen would serve as volunteers. I was always involved in the softball games. I will never forget the day when nuns from the local Catholic Church had too much to drink and started acting in surprising ways.

Never in those days was there any fear of strangers. We never even locked our house or car. As a child I got up in the morning and was outside playing most of the day. I remember the horse and wagon coming down the street twice weekly to deliver fresh fruits and vegetables. Milk and soda was delivered right to your door, and every month or so the knife and tool sharpener would come along in his work van. I have to give a special mention to the Good Humor man. He knew every child's name, and I remember him giving one child, who didn't have money, a free ice cream cone. Times were so different and I miss them. We may not have had video games, cell phones, and Facebook to occupy out time, but we had stickball, punch ball, handball, hopscotch, jump rope etc. We learned to interact face to face and I believe were much better off for it.

In today's world parents make play dates for their children. In my day children made their own fun. It wasn't always the best. For example, one neighbor had a coal-fired furnace and once my friends and I slid down the coal chute into the bin. We got so dirty. We were kids and always into new adventures. When I was old enough, about age eight, my friends and I would ride our bikes along the Belt Parkway Bike Path to Rockaway Beach. I don't know the mileage exactly but it had to be more than ten miles. In today's day and age parents are afraid to let their children out of their sight. This is such a shame. My house was located on a canal, and so in the summer we swam and fished right off our back yard. I will never forget the day when I was seven years old and decided to go fishing by myself. I baited a hook and cast out into the middle of the canal. All of a sudden the fishing pole bent hard. I had something big on the line. I struggled, but reeled in the fish. It turned out to be a large eel. It looked just like a snake. I looked on horrified, as it seemed to be slithering towards me. I dropped the fishing pole and ran into the house. My brother came out and threw the eel back into the water. That night I had a nightmare of the eel. I dreamt that it was slithering towards me, and as it got closer my heart started to race.

Fishing is a good example for how things have changed. During the summer months Snappers (baby blue fish) came into the bays. As a child I didn't have money to go to a bait and tackle shop. We had to be creative in the 1950's. I took an old screen. Broke off the edges and tied string to the outer four corners, and then to each other. Next, a piece of bread was wet and broke into small pieces. I went down the ladder from my house to the water, and lowered the screen with the bread into the water. In a few minutes small bait fish would attack the bread. The screen was lifted and I had bait to fish. It was a different world.

My father's mother lived in the house with us. She was a Norwegian woman who spent her days alone in her room. She ate by herself and socialized only with two of our neighbors who were also Norwegian. The only time I remember her speaking with me was when she asked me to go to the store to buy her butter pecan ice cream. When I returned home she let me have a little of it with her.

When I was eight years old one day I came home from school and my parents told me to wait outside. I didn't understand why, but do remember seeing strangers coming and going from the house. My grandmother had died of a heart attack. This was my first encounter with death, and led to an emotional change in me. Up until then I had been a happy child busy roller skating and playing much of the day with friends and cousins who lived nearby. After my grandmothers' death, for the first time, I began obsessing about dying. I would lie awake at night and wonder what happens after death. The idea of losing my personality forever frightened me horribly. My heart would pound through my chest and I couldn't sleep. This I never told anyone. Growing up my mother had taught me two prayers, and I added to these with my own prayers. Shortly after my grandmothers death I suddenly developed a strange habit. This is a habit that I am sure many will relate to in their own lives, maybe not the same habit, but something similar. It is a childish defense mechanism. When I said my prayers if I happened to make a mistake I would stop and start from the beginning again. You can imagine the pressure I put on myself as I neared the end of my prayers. There were nights when I had said my prayers five or six times before getting them perfectly uttered. As a psychologist I recognize this as a superstitious way of warding off harm coming to those I loved. Fortunately for me this obsessive-compulsive trait didn't carry over to my adulthood. In my practice I saw adults whose very lives were hounded by such fears. One woman would stop in the street whenever she saw something shiny such as tinfoil. She had to check to make sure it didn't contain her personal information on it. If her husband was driving along and she spotted something shiny in the road she would make him stop. If he didn't she would become hysterical. Such cases of severe obsessive-compulsive disorder are one of the reasons for people being declared totally disabled by the Social Security Administration. Like most things there are silver linings. People with mild obsessive-compulsive traits tend to be some of the most successful and creative people around. Attention to detail and perfectionistic tendencies are the reasons why.

What helped me cope with my fears and also ill health was reading in bed with a flashlight. Lucky Star and the Space Rangers was a series of books that I loved. My parents knew of my interest in space and brought me a map of the solar system that was put up on my ceiling. This began my interest in science. I would lie there and imagine flying through space in a rocket ship. I learned the sizes of each of the planets, and their distance from the sun. I had two close friends my neighbor Steve and my cousin Bobby. Both were a little younger than me. When I was eleven and Steve ten his parents bought him a telescope. Every night for that summer we would take turns looking at the moon and stars. I was fascinated by the universe and tried to imagine how it came into being.

I attended the local public school P.S. 277. This was a neighborhood only school. There were three classes for each grade. I was always in the top class, and each year, from kindergarten through sixth grade, it was almost always the same children in my class. I knew everyone by name and we were like a family. Mathematics was my favorite subject. I remember in the sixth grade sitting at my desk and computing the distance light traveled in one year, and we didn't have calculators. Things like this fascinated me. Right alongside the school was a large playground. Everything from swings, slides and monkey bars to basketball, baseball and handball courts. Starting at about age eight or nine I literally lived in the playground. In the summer, weekends, and even after school, a group of us would meet to play stickball, or basketball, or handball. We would decide each day what game to play. Some days we would play one sport in the morning and another in the afternoon. Childhood was wonderful and innocent.

Religion I haven't mentioned for a reason. It played a very small role in my life. My father never went to church. Once we convinced him to come to Christmas Eve service with my mother and me. He fell asleep during the service and began snoring. It was so embarrassing. My father was an only child, but my mother had one brother and four sisters who made it to adulthood, and all but one lived nearby. She had several more siblings but they had died during childhood. My mother was raised Roman Catholic and did attend church when younger, but then one day was turned off to religion. I was the only one of my siblings she told the story to. She mentioned that when my sister and brother were small two nuns from the local Catholic Church visited. They asked her if she planned on raising the children Roman Catholic. My mother responded of course. The nuns then told her we know your husband is Lutheran, and if you are worried that he might get upset and hurt you we have ways to ensure that he never finds out. My mother told me she was shocked and angry. Her words to them were "*you call yourself nuns and you want me to keep things from my husband get out.*" She raised her children Lutheran and I know it did cause her mother a problem. I saw that my grandmother favored her other children over my mother, and I think this was the reason why. I was put into Sunday school in the third grade because my cousin Bobby was also going to be attending. I still get teary eyed when I think of him. Bobby went on a Boy Scout camping trip to upstate New York when he was age ten or eleven. They were canoeing and the water was supposedly more rapid than they had expected. The canoe turned over and Bobby drowned. It took two weeks for them to find his body. My fear of death and panic attacks blossomed once more. Now that I am older and have children of my own I can imagine the incredible emotional pain his parents must have felt.

When I was around age thirteen one day it suddenly hit me. If we are all going to die one day then why waste time worrying about it. The time should be spent enjoying life. I guess I was destined to become a psychologist. With this new insight my panic attacks slowed for a time, but only for a time. Eventually a crisis would occur in my life to kick them back into high gear.

Before encountering the crisis there was one incident I remember clearly that supports my eventual career choice. One day we had just finished playing a ball game. Most people left. My neighbor Joey, who was two years older than me, and I were the only one's remaining. I was twelve and he fourteen. He seemed upset about something. I asked him if he was okay. He responded not really. I asked if he wanted to talk about it. Joe went on for quite awhile about problems he was having at home. He then stopped and looked at me and said, *"there is something different and special about you."*

The summer I had graduated from elementary school began a change in my life that, unfortunately, was not for the better. My sister had married when I was nine years old, and moved to upstate New York. Her husband Bob was an electrical engineer who eventually received a promotion to manager of IBM's new research facilities in North Carolina. They moved there when I was thirteen. My brother, and his friends were obsessed with their cars and were always working to make them go faster. Gerritsen Beach was a fishing village and the social center was a bar called the Tamaqua located at the main fishing boat dock. Nighttime's my brother and his friends could be found there drinking, playing shuffle board, and socializing. I do remember fondly that he would sometimes take me to the movies or bowling. One evening we were outside having a football catch. I was about ten years old. He threw a bullet pass which I caught but at the expense of dislocating my thumb. We came inside and called our local doctor. Dr. Baronberg was the epitome of an old fashioned doctor, and one I wish we still had. His office hours were over for the day but he had left his home number for emergencies. We called and he gave us his home address and said come on over. We got there as he was finishing dinner. The doctor took me into his home office and proceeded to pop my thumb back into place. Today's doctors would simply say go to the emergency room. The most positive thing in my brother's life was his girlfriend Peggy. They had been dating from the time she was thirteen and he sixteen. Peggy was pretty and such a pleasant person to be around. Unfortunately the negative side of religion once again reared its ugly head. At age twenty-two my brother asked Peggy's family for her hand in marriage. Her parents said only if you convert to Roman Catholicism. This caused conflict and the two broke up. I was shocked that a relationship could be destroyed over something like religion. After all they were both Christian religions. My brother was devastated. He was vulnerable and on the rebound he began seeing a girl from the block I lived on. She was a girl who wanted to get out of her house. My brother ended up getting her pregnant and my mother told him he had to marry her. It turned out that she was neither a good wife nor a good mother. The next year his second child was born. Two years later they divorced. My brother was given full custody of his daughter and son. He moved his family into my maternal grandmother's home. She was a good woman but spoke only Polish. I believe his living there gave her company and my brother would help out at home during the evenings. After three years my brother and his ex-wife reconciled for the children's sake, and moved to Long Island. No sooner did they get there then she started cheating with the real estate agent that had sold them their house. My brother ended up throwing her out. Interestingly wherever he has moved in his life she moved nearby. To his credit he never told his children to dislike her and he helped her when she asked. Now that she is older she regrets her past. Today he lives in Florida with his second wife Judy and is happy. The important thing was that with my brother and sister away from home by the time I was thirteen I was ripe for what would happen the next year.

TROUBLED TEENS

By the time I was a teenager Gerritsen Beach had become largely an Irish and Italian area. Most people were civil service workers. Police, Fire, Transit and Sanitation workers predominated. Drinking was a big problem, but hadn't impacted my life just yet.

I will never forget one night when I was twelve. My two cousins and I developed a new game. The corner house near my cousin Ralph's had hedges surrounding it. We would run across the street and jump over the hedges. On my second or third jump the back of my foot hit the hedges and I fell face forward into the pointed cement blocks at the base of her house. I lay there for several seconds until my cousins Bill and Ralph came to help me up. I had a nasty cut on the left side of my skull, and was bleeding profusely. My aunt cleaned the cut and bandaged me up. My parents took me to Dr. Baronberg who recleaned the cut and gave me a butterfly stitch to close the wound. He told my parents to watch me closely for a few days. Another time that same year I was riding my bike fast down the street. A car was coming towards me, and so I moved closer to the parked cars. Just as I was passing a parked car a woman threw open her drivers side door. I hit the door, went flying over the hood of her car, and landed in the street on my head. Twice in one year I had luckily survived head injuries. The damage I sustained to my neck would however come back to hound me in the future.

September 1959 marked my first day in Marine Park Junior High School. I will never forget my first day there. I arrived early to school. The building was huge. It was so much bigger than my elementary school. The students were milling around outside the building in the large schoolyard. I looked but didn't see anyone from elementary school. When I got to my homeroom class I didn't know anyone there. I was scared and felt kind of like a little fish in a huge pond. Things were worst for me because I was shy until I got to know people. I was so comfortable in elementary school. I knew everyone in my class, and saw them around the neighborhood. I had never seen these people before in my life. I wasn't happy. It turned out that there were thirty-two seventh grade classes. The one thing that made the year bearable for me was that during the year they arranged a basketball tournament for each grade. Sports were such a big part of my life before then that I joined the team. We had five players, and two of them were really good. The rest of us were not bad either. My class won every game, and classmates came out to see the final game. This gave me a sense of accomplishment and classmates congratulated me. Sports were a blessing for me, and have continued to be. My grades that year were good, but this would change.

Eighth grade began with me again not knowing anyone in my class. This year there was no basketball tournament to help me get to know my classmates, and there was one student who, for some reason, seemed not to like me. Possibly he chose me because I was tall, and lanky and he felt I was an easy target to pick on. My mother left the house at five thirty a.m. to meet her carpool and get taken to work at Sperry Gyroscope in Long Island. My father was a baker who worked from seven a.m. until three thirty p.m. for Larsen's Bakery in northern Brooklyn. That year my Polish grandmother would come to my house to see me off to school. She would then go home or to one of my aunt's nearby homes. She would return at three p.m. to let me in the house, and stay with me until my parents came home. I hated school and so began cutting out. I would leave the house in the morning and go into the cellar door that I had opened. When my grandmother left I would go upstairs and watch television or play basketball with a hoop that I attached to the back of a door frame. I would then get back into the basement just before three p.m. When notes came to the house about my absences my grandmother didn't read English and so I would tear them up. Towards the end of the year I would make an effort to go to school and I would usually pass subjects but barely so.

CRISIS 1

It was late the next year that my world turned upside down, and I slid down a path that could have destroyed my life permanently. The ninth grade started off on a positive note. I did have two friends in the class from elementary school. Eddie ended up being in my wedding party nineteen years later, and Susan was very friendly. The class was put together a few weeks into the school year. It appears that the administration had created a class of students who it was felt had potential, but were not living up to it. The teacher, Mrs. Saltzman, was a lawyer who had made the decision to give up law and return to her true love of teaching. One month into the year she did something that endeared her to the students. One of the boys had gotten into an argument with a teacher that could have led to his being suspended. Mrs. Saltzman went to the principal and stuck up for her student. Apparently she told the principal that the teacher had badly overreacted and this was the cause of the confrontation. The student was not suspended, and the class looked at our teacher with respect and treated her that way also. There was another special thing about this school year that made me want to come to school. Mr. Meizel was our science teacher. This man was blessed with an ability to reach students. Every week he would perform another science experiment in class. From childhood I had been interested in science. Mr. Meizel awakened that interest. At the end of the school year the school held an awards ceremony. The best student from each class in every major subject was presented with an award. I received awards for science and mathematics. My parents were both there to see me receive the awards. This was my proudest accomplishment throughout my school career. Unfortunately it did not last because the first crisis was about to begin and my life changed horribly. It began with a disabling illness, and the severe disruption it caused my family.

My mother was such a special person. I can only imagine the life she led. She was raised on a farm in Connecticut. She told me that at the age of six she and her older sister Dorothy, who suffered from polio, would travel to school by horseback. On the way to school the girls would stop to deliver milk and eggs to neighbors. My mother left school after the eighth grade to work and help her family. Actually my father did the same thing. This was not unusual as the depression years reportedly saw many children leaving school early to help their families. Gerritsen Beach, where they both grew up as teenagers was a haven for bootleggers. My father lived on the water and he told me that bootlegger's owned the house next door. Reportedly it was the mobster Lucky Luciano's gang. They called him lucky because of all the times he had escaped attempts on his life. I remember my father telling me the story of his father coming home from work and shining the car lights on the basement of the neighbor's house. He thought he saw my father in the basement. My grandfather reportedly got out of his car and peeked in the window. He saw my father playing cards with the bootleggers. My father was sixteen at the time. They were playing cards while they waited for a shipment to arrive. My granddad, who died when I was a baby, went in, took my father out and gave him the beating of his life. Thankfully my father never ventured near that house again. My mother's house was located exactly one block from the water. Her house was reportedly riddled with bullets when the police had set a trap for bootleggers and a firefight ensued. It was definitely an exciting and very dangerous time to be living in Gerritsen.

Getting back to my mother, she was the rock of our family. She left the house early every morning to work in Long Island. When she came home she cooked dinner and then cleaned the house. My father was an only child and he was spoiled. He let my mother do all chores. My mother's life was her family. As a result she had only two good friends, one from work who lived in Long Island and the other, my godmother Betty, who lived in Gerritsen Beach. The summer before I began high school my mother had a major heart attack. She was forty-three years old. Fortunately she survived, but the rest of her life was hampered by multiple medical complications. Her life had turned upside down and she struggled to accept it. If she had supportive friends nearby I believe it would have been different for her. Now that I am older and wiser I understand how depressed she became. My mother's way of coping with her depression was to turn to liquor. Both of my parents, especially my father, were drinkers. I never saw them drunk however. Within one year my mother was drinking one quart of Vodka each day. My father also began drinking heavier. I knew they loved each other, and never remember them fighting before this. Alcohol changed all that. My brother and sister were out of the house and so I was alone to see and hear the arguing. The fighting never became physical but viciously verbal at times. Whenever I pleaded with them to stop I was told to go to bed or just stay out of it. Many a night when I was fourteen I cried myself to sleep. After awhile I came up with an idea to slow their drinking. Every night after they had gone to bed I would put two ounces of water into their liquor bottles. One day my father caught on to my plan. *"Are you messing with my whiskey; it tastes like water?"* Of course I denied it, but he knew. Never again did he say anything, but never again did I mess with their liquor. Instead I found a new way to cope. It started out harmlessly, but would escalate, and almost end up killing me.

That year my one good friend Wally had moved to California, but before he moved he introduced me to a group of his friends that he would hang out with at times. I was shy while he was handsome and not at all shy. Girls liked him. When he moved I continued to hang out nights with this group. That year things were good. At nights we would hang out behind the Tamaqua, listen to music and talk. Some days we would go over some one's house and do the same. Eventually couples started forming and kissing became a pastime. I knew one girl named Patty seemed to like me, but I was much too shy to approach her. I remember the boys I hung with would do things like climb into people's yards and steal apples or pears from their trees. It was wrong but childishly wrong. Soon things would change for the worse. You can guess the cause.

High school was another nightmare for me. Sheepshead Bay High School was a large school with over four thousand students. Once again I knew no one in most of my classes. By this time my parent's lives revolved around alcohol. I could come home at three a.m. in the morning and no one knew that I had been out late. There was no such thing anymore as parental guidance. I was totally on my own.

The year before we had been stealing apples, and acting like children without parental guidance. By the time I hit high school my group of "friends" had started drinking. Getting beer or alcohol in Gerritsen Beach was simple. I wasn't the only one with alcoholic parents who also had no one watching over them. By age sixteen we were going into two of the local bars and getting served. By age sixteen I was also working afternoons and Saturdays for International Telephone and Telegraph in Manhattan. My job was to deliver telegrams, mostly to lawyers or businesses, and most of these were located in the Empire State Building. High school became an afterthought. Most days a few of us would meet over one person's home in the morning. His parents were at work. The home was not big and the furniture old, but they had a well stocked bar. We would sit around and drink for an hour or so, and then get to school and hour or two late. Rarely did I ever do homework. The only class that I always excelled at was gym. Every year the gym teacher would assign me as a floor leader. If the lesson for the day were basketball, performing pushups, or working the parallel bars, I would be assigned to teach a group of students how to do the lesson correctly. Gym was the only class that I always received an "A" in. I eventually graduated with a 69 average and a general diploma. Academic diplomas were for people expected to attend college. Commercial diplomas were for people desiring a skill to work in an office. A general diploma was for those who had no idea what they wished to do, or just lacked ability. At that time the former of these was obviously I. Never, in my house, was the idea of going to college discussed. You finished high school and then went to work.

If I had gone to college it would have been a waste of time and money.

MY DOWNFALL

By the time I turned sixteen everything changed. The 1960's were beginning to bloom and with it a drug culture. My first experience was when a group of us, male and female, were in a friend's yard sitting around a table and smoking marijuana through a water pipe. Now my asthma was still an issue but much less so than when I was younger, and so I joined in. The marijuana did not hurt my lungs at all, but I did not like the way it made me feel. Due to the fact that the marijuana did not hurt my lungs, and all of the boys and girls I was hanging out with smoked, I thought maybe I too could smoke and fit in better. I inhaled just once. My lungs burned horribly, and I coughed, and thought all those ads about the dangers of smoking must be true.

I may never have smoked and did not like marijuana, but we were at the stage of experimenting with other drugs. Robitussion AC, a cough medicine with codeine, and barbiturates taken together became the craze. It became my nightly high for the next several years. I do remember that when I was about twenty years old barbiturates suddenly became hard to get. A subset of the group, not at all very nice people, started to shoot up heroin. They began robbing drug stores at night. I was told they got in through air conditioning ducts. One day they were a man short for a job, and asked me to join them for that night's work. I didn't hesitate one second. No way////. They called me a pansy, but I paid them no mind. I didn't mind taking drugs that had been stolen, but drew a line in the sand. I still didn't get it that by buying stolen drugs I was supporting thieves, but my morals would not let me steal. Actually once when I was thirteen I had stolen a magazine from the local candy store. I stole it because I didn't think they would let me buy it. Yes, it was a girly magazine. This hounded me for years. One day when I was in my late twenties I drove back to the candy store to leave money for the magazine I had taken, but the store was closed.

I must admit that one time I did join in with five other guys and mainlined heroin. It is now more than forty-five years later and I still can remember the incredible feeling of intense warmth spreading throughout my body. That night I swore to myself that I would never do such a thing again. I realized that this drug was dangerous, and could see how easily it was to become a slave to it. Fortunately for me I have strong willpower and never went near heroin again.

Unfortunately, I was addicted to taking Robitussion AC and barbiturates and continued these drugs. Now that I am older and wiser I realize that I was attracted to these specific drugs because they numbed the emotional pain I was feeling at home. I also realized that I could no longer stay with the so-called friends I had as their lives were becoming more and more dysfunctional. The one friend that I remained in contact with throughout the years was Michael Murdock. Like me Mike was on the fringes of the crowd. He worked for years after school and on weekends in Sid's deli on Gerritsen Avene. Mike was the first person I knew who went to college. He eventually became a police captain. As we got older we would speak a few times a year. Mike would tell me of all the "quote" friends we had who had died or were in jail. One person was even living in an abandoned car in the back weeds of Gerritsen Beach. Drugs destroyed so many lives. Mike spent a lot of time helping out after 9-11. The last time I saw him was at his son's funeral. His son had a seizure disorder. One night, while asleep, he had a seizure and vomited during it. When I saw Mike he himself was on oxygen, and his organs were beginning to fail. He was sure all the 9-11 work he did was the reason for his medical condition. I was unable to attend his funeral but he remains in my prayers. Michael Murdock was one of the good ones.

Besides Mike most others from my past were cut off. I cut the amount of drugs I was taking in half for two weeks. The amount of drugs I was taking was still pretty high. I then went cold turkey. For approximately two weeks I suffered horrible headaches and was vomiting daily. By this time I was working on Wall Street, and was unable to go in to work while withdrawing. The doctor I went to thought it was the flu and gave me a note for work. After two weeks it was over. What wasn't over was that my whole social life revolved around new friends who were taking drugs. Wall Street was rampant with drug use at that time.

Around that time Timothy Leary was expounding the positive qualities of the drug LSD. Lysergic Acid Diethylamide was a powerful hallucinogenic drug that became a craze. A few of the people I knew were experimenting with this drug, and so I joined them. The very first time I took LSD I ran home, put a pillow over my head, and prayed it would go away. A thousand thoughts and insights were racing through my head every second. Hours later it stopped. I thought about the experience. If I could learn to control it, as Leary had said was possible, it must be amazing. The next twenty times I took it I worked on controlling the experience. It was an amazing drug. Your senses were heightened immensely. Once, I was wearing a short sleeve shirt and for at least an hour sat and stared at an aura that was raised about two inches above my arms. It was a shimmering wave that was silver in color with a bluish tinge. I know now of people who can see and even read aura's without drugs. I only wish I could do so. Unfortunately everything was not all positive. One morning while I was in bed I began seizing. Later on I found out that I went into seizure on and off all that day. I awoke in a hospital. At a later date my parents told me that the doctors thought I might die, and if I did survive there would probably be brain damage. I was put through two weeks of torturous tests. I will never forget lying on a table with a machine above me. I was injected with a substance into my artery that made me go into seizures. The whole time I was seizing they took pictures of my brain. They never found a reason for the seizures and so labeled them idiopathic. I knew the reason. I had taken LSD a few nights before the seizures, and had what was termed a bad trip. I never figured out why they hadn't found it in my blood.

The recuperation period was long. For weeks I needed to be in a room shielded from any sound. Any noise caused migraines. My right arm, where they had injected drugs into my artery, remained swollen for months. Once I had recovered I began going out again. I got a new job working for a watch company in midtown Manhattan. Henry, a man of about sixty and I, handled all the mail. People would send watches and clocks to be repaired. We would parcel these out to the workers assigned to repair them, and then ship them out when fixed. I loved this job because so many of the workers were young Hispanic women and they would flirt with me. It never went beyond flirting but it was a boost to a weak self-esteem. Unfortunately, by nights I was still hanging out with some of the same group of "friends", and once again began using my usual drugs, but much less so. Never again did I go near LSD. I was frightened to death of it now. Within one year a friend had told me about an opening at the American Stock Exchange. I applied for the job and got it. Now I had dreams of being a millionaire by the time I was forty. I quickly moved up in position. Within one year I was promoted to reporter on the trading floor and got to know some high-powered brokers. I also observed some of the shenanigans that went on with trading stocks. Once again I was confronted, with an environment where drugs were plentiful. I had been doing good cutting down my usage but now saw it beginning to rise up once more. After three and one-half years on the trading floor the country went into a deep recession. The exchange offered me a job, but it required a demotion. My pride got in the way. I applied and was offered a supervisory position at Dean Witter Brokerage. This turned out to be a great decision because I came to hate the job within less than one year. I had eight clerks under me. All but one was a minority and all around my age. The other supervisors were considerably older. The first time I was called into the manager's office was because I had figured out a more efficient way for my clerks to handle an aspect of the job. It led to fewer errors that had to be corrected. The manager told me *"what do you think you're doing? We have procedures here and you can't change them."* I tried to show him the benefit of the change I had made but to no avail. Several months later I was called in again. This time the manager told me *"we know you are bright, but you will never go anywhere in this company"*. I said I don't understand. His response to me was *"that is the problem you do not understand, and probably never will."* I thought about this long and hard and finally got it. The other supervisors all ate lunch everyday with the manager. All but one of them was white. I ate lunch everyday with the clerks that worked for me. All but one of them was a minority. I never had been confronted with outright bigotry in my life. To me people were people. Friendly people you liked. Unfriendly people you didn't. This woke me up. I realized that I had to make big changes to my life, <u>and it had to start with me.</u>

MY AWAKENING

Once again I weaned myself off drugs. This time would be different because I realized that I could never go back to hanging with any of my old friends. I knew I had to find a new way to occupy my time positively. I developed a plan. I have always been excellent at developing and sticking to plans. I enrolled at Brooklyn College nights as a non-matriculated student. My high school average in no way entitled me to be matriculated or degree bound. I received a shock. I had enrolled for one reason, to change my life and avoid temptation, but soon found another. I quickly realized that I loved learning and everything came easily to me. I was like a sponge. After completing sixteen credits of mostly "A" grades they matriculated me and I no longer had to pay tuition. If only we had those days now. Friday nights I used to go over to my uncle George's house and play board games with his three younger daughters. This I remember as a good time. Never again in my life have I used an illegal drug, and I will only have one drink at a wedding or other occasion. I had survived the first major crisis point in my life, and have since counseled many others that the way to break alcohol or drug addiction is to avoid all negative influences and occupy your time totally and positively. Asking God for help is a good way to reinforce your motivation as well. As I began starting my new life I did much soul searching. I realized that I was angry with my parents for becoming alcoholics and for emotionally abandoning me. I then saw how I had fallen into a horrible mess because of my need to be accepted. I took responsibility. I forgave my parents and began pitying them instead. I knew they were kind and loving people and my childhood could not have been better. Alcohol was a demon that ruined their lives. My mother ended up bleeding uncontrollably from cirrhosis at the age of fifty-eight. The doctors performed emergency surgery and gave her five years to live. They were right. She died at age sixty-three of a massive stroke. My father was lost without her. He had retired at age sixty-two to take care of her, and all of his friends were from work. The remainder of his life he did crossword puzzles in the morning, and was an avid reader. He went to the bar after lunch and again around four p.m. After dinner he watched television and had a few drinks. He passed at age seventy-five.

Once I had let go of my anger towards my parents, and taken responsibility for my life things really began to change for the better. It was as if a tremendous weight had been taken from me. By the third year of college I had decided to major in psychology. A friend from college convinced me to first become a school psychologist, as we would be guaranteed jobs. This was due to the hiring freeze that had gone on in N.Y.C. for several years, and the openings that would be awaiting us when it finished. She was right. For my last school year I needed to go to college by day to take certain prerequisites. I gladly left Wall Street and got a job twenty-five hours a week working in a drug store near the college. It was me and the pharmacist half the week and the pharmacist and another student the rest of the week. Ben was a good man, and he encouraged me to go on to graduate school. I will never forget that he was the only one to give me a graduation gift.

Going to school fulltime days was eye opening. Night students, coming from work, were all serious students. Day students I saw smoking pot on the campus green. The difference was unbelievable. Fortunately I was only taking advanced classes at this time, and the students in these classes were serious. One of my professors in psychology gave me permission to take a graduate class in psychopharmacology. In this class were pre-med students and graduate students in experimental psychology. I truly loved science and aced the course.

In 1974 I graduated Magna Cum Laude with honors in psychology and was accepted to the Brooklyn College School Psychology Program. The program was exceptional. The head of the program, Max Siegel, had been President of the American Psychological Association. His assistant, Laura Barbanel, was President of the New York State Psychological Association, and the other professors were superb as well. The atmosphere of the program was friendly. Towards the end of my first year I was required to administer The Wechsler Adult Intelligence Test to a senior citizen. My father was 67 years old and agreed. He had an eighth grade education and drank much of his life, but still scored 120. This score is considered to be in the superior range of intelligence. I can only imagine if things had been different for him. For the two years I was there I grew as a person and made quality friends. The second year in the program we were required to participate in group counseling. The woman professor who taught counseling led the group. Half the class was in each group. This was an amazing experience for me. Never before had I opened up and shared personal information with a supportive group of friends. By the end of the year we had bonded and helped each other grow as individuals.

By this time I was in my late twenties, and realized there was still one change that I needed to make. Shyness had to go. At night they offered a continuing education class in dance. Fortunately it was at a time that I didn't have a class. The Latin Hustle was being taught. Saturday night fever was the craze. I took the class and was decent at it. The instructor told me after the final class that he gave private lessons. A few of us took him up on this. His sister was his assistant. It turned out that I was the best of his students, and his sister and I would demonstrate steps for the others. This was another major self-esteem boost. Today I don't remember one single step.

Upon graduation I was accepted into the Ph.D. Program at the City University of New York Graduate School. I did have other options but this was a school that I could easily afford. It turned out to be an excellent choice. The first year we chose one of four majors within the program. I was already a school psychologist and so needed only a few classes to fulfill that major. Therefore I picked a second major area to study. I turned out to be the only student from my year who chose statistics and research design as my major. I didn't realize it at the time, but most of New York City's research institutes were located inside the same building. Every year I was hired to work as a research assistant on a project. The pay more than covered my tuition. Additionally, I even was given my own office within the school. It was tiny, but it was mine. I was elected as student representative to the Graduate Program Council, and the two professors in the area of statistics and research design were at my disposal since I was the only student who chose this major. To top it off I was invited along to attend research and educational conferences with the faculty. I absolutely loved this, and considered this as a career path. Imagine going to a first rate hotel, having excellent meals, and playing pingpong at midnight with my advisor. The one drawback to my schooling was that your doctoral advisor had the right to decide if you required additional coursework to supplement your training. After I had completed all required coursework my advisor required me to take two calculus classes at Hunter College and a third course at Baruch by a visiting professor specializing in test design. He told me *"this is called rites of passage. We had to go through it and so do you."*

BEST DECISION I EVER MADE

At the end of the first semester we had to take examinations in eight areas of psychology, statistics, research design, developmental psychology, etc. As soon as I had passed these I embarked on my next goal. I knew that I wanted to be married and have a family. On Friday nights at eleven p.m., I would get dressed up, and go to a discotheque in Bay Ridge. It was named the Gazebo. This was a new experience and definitely not in my comfort zone at first. I quickly learned that girls standing around by themselves were looking to meet someone. The first time I went I spotted a tall, pretty girl standing by herself, and so went up to her, said hello, and asked if she would like to dance. She said yes. We danced, and when the music stopped she walked away from me. I didn't know the appropriate thing to do. She walked away. Should I go after her? I didn't, but later on that night I asked another girl to dance and she didn't leave when the music stopped. We talked for a while, and I got her phone number. The next week I took her to dinner. At dinner, as we talked, I was questioning in my mind if this person was the one who had the qualities I would want for a wife and mother of my children. Gosh I was so analytical. She turned out to be a secretary who did not have interests that I did and was not for me. The next two girls I had picked up were also not what I was looking for. And then it happened. I returned to the disco, and there she was. The tall, pretty girl I had met the first time I was there. I went right up to her and asked her to dance. When the music ended I grabbed her hand and told her I would like to get to know you better. We sat down, ordered one drink, and spent two hours talking. Doreen was everything I was looking for. She was a kindergarten teacher, loved children, was close to her family, and was tall and pretty besides. She had come with a friend and left with her. By our first date I hoped that one day she would be my wife. We were inseparable during the time we dated. I would go over to her house shortly after I had gotten home from work or school and eaten. I was a little worried since she was Greek and I had heard stories from friends about Greeks making their children marry other Greeks. Fortunately my future mother in law liked me. It is now thirty-four years later and I still am in love. Doreen was raised Greek Orthodox and her family was actively involved with their church. For the next 29 years we went weekly to church as a family. I felt early on that the Greek Orthodox Churches we attended were more concerned with nationalism and being Greek than they were with religion. In the church we attended in New Jersey I ran the basketball team for men, and on Sunday's the coffee hour for the community. Rarely did I ever go into the church itself. The church made me feel more distanced from God than I had been in the past.

I finished school (at least the course work) and quickly got a job as a school psychologist for the N.Y.C. Board of Education. It turned out that one of the doctoral students that I had been tutoring in statistics was the regional director of all clinical services in Brooklyn. It's whom you know and always has been. This job was perfect for me. The workload wasn't great that first year, but it gave me access to the data on which I eventually wrote my doctoral dissertation. At the time bias in intelligence testing was a big issue. I compared black and white high school students on the Wechsler Adult Intelligence Scale. I utilized the very latest statistical models to test for bias, and came up with a unique idea for matching groups of students on other measures of intelligence first. My findings were superb and my advisor wanted me to write up two papers for professional journals.

Unfortunately, I never did write the papers. The only bias I found was in the subtests that offered bonus points for rapid performance. Placing multicolored blocks into patterns and arranging pictures in an order that told a story are two examples. On these subtests whites received significantly more bonus points than did blacks. I explained this using a learned helplessness model. I wonder if those results would still hold today. One year after getting my doctoral degree and completing the supervision requirement, I passed the psychologist licensing examination, and started a part-time private practice. I knew if I were going to be helpful to these patients I would have to go for additional training. When I first received my doctorate in psychology and before applying for my license to practice privately I enrolled in the Institute for Rational Emotive Psychotherapy. The father of cognitive behavioral psychotherapy ran the institute. Albert Ellis was a character if ever you have met one. Soon after meeting him he explained to his new students how he had developed the concept of cognitive behavioral psychotherapy. I mention it here because it clearly makes the point that so many breakthroughs, not only in science, are made by individuals who suddenly have an epiphany. I'm also relating it because it made us all laugh. Ellis told us that he was a trained psychoanalyst, but by his late twenties still had not had sex with a woman. He became interested in the writings of noted behaviorists such as Watson and Skinner, and figured why not give it a try. Ellis therefore designed his own behavior modification program. He decided that every weekend in the summer he would go to the Brooklyn Botanical Gardens and force himself to sit down next to a young woman and try to strike up a conversation. Note that Ellis was tall, lanky and not exactly handsome. Fear of rejection was always an issue for him. He told us that the first ten women to reject his advances made him feel awful. When the second ten rejected him he didn't feel so awful. By the third ten to reject him he was beginning to look at things as if it was a game. By the fourth ten to reject him he didn't feel bad at all. Albert told us that it was literally the forty-ninth woman who agreed to go with him for coffee, and that night was the first time for him. It was only afterwards that he thought of the whole situation, and realized that he had desensitized himself to an irrational fear, the fear being that it is so horrible to be rejected. In actuality the women who rejected his advances tended to be quite nice about it. On the basis of this personal experience he developed a theory (cognitive behavioral psychotherapy) that has become the most widespread theory of psychotherapy. Ellis taught us that irrational thinking leads to disturbed behaviors and the job of the therapist was to identify and ultimately correct the irrational thinking. I was to read later on how scientists such as Newton and Einstein also had such personal epiphanies. Often these epiphanies came about when the person was dreaming. More on lucid dreaming will be discussed later.

Things were moving nicely. My first assignment in the school system was at two high schools. James Madison was only blocks away from my house, and George Wingate, which was an all minority school, in East Flatbush near Crown Heights Brooklyn. This school was quite a distance from where I lived. Doreen and I had married six months after I started working, and I couldn't have been happier. My wife stayed home and raised the three children we eventually had. Christina, Maria and Thomas were a blessing. I finally had the family, and love, that I had always yearned for. The following September I was asked to choose which of the two schools I would like to work at full time. It took me about a nanosecond to choose Wingate. Wingate may have been a tough school with a bad reputation, but the staff stuck closely together, and when I started the principal shook my hand and said I'm grateful for any help you can give us. In later years he used to slip and call me his son's name. The reason for this was my ability to calm sticky situations. Whenever he was having a suspense hearing and the family became argumentative and brought up the black-white issue the principal would tell the guidance counselor to call me in. I had a knack for calming even the stickiest situations.

A few years after I started working a student committed suicide on the athletic field of James Madison High School. A suicide prevention team was formed for Brooklyn high schools. I was asked to join the team. My responsibility was educational. I spoke at clinical staff development days about how to identify the signs of suicidal ideology, and available resources in the community. I also went into schools that had invited me to speak to the entire faculty. In doing so I developed a reputation and was written up in a local newspaper. The suicide prevention team was eventually changed to a crisis response team. My very first intern, Brian Utnick, joined a social worker and me. For the next ten years we would go into schools where a student had been murdered. I ended up having gone into most high schools in Brooklyn for this purpose. My job was to counsel the friends of the murdered student, and also keep my ears open for possible retaliation. The very first school I was asked to go into was Thomas Jefferson High School. I got the call in the afternoon. Two students had been shot dead, and they would like me there as soon as possible. Fortunately, Jefferson was only twenty minutes away from my school. When I was within a block of the school I got a surprise. Awaiting me were news trucks and reporters. The next morning African American men in military garb were patrolling the halls. The police commissioner was there, and the school was awaiting Al Sharpton and Jessie Jackson. Luckily for me I was able to avoid all the political posturing going on. I was given an office to see students in. From them I learned that one student had just gotten out of jail, and he swore that he would kill the student who had "ratted" him out to the police. The other student heard he was in danger, and decided that he would kill the other before he himself was killed. He brought a gun to school, and waited outside a classroom the victim was in. When the person walked out of the classroom with a friend the both of them were shot dead. Over the years I eventually was sent to most high schools in my district that consisted of half of Brooklyn. In every case but one it was a matter of one gang member murdering another gang member. The one exception was my own school. One day a friend asked a very popular student if he would drive him somewhere. The friend went into a house to reportedly get some money owed him. Suddenly the friend came running to the car. A man with a shotgun was chasing him. Both students were shot dead. There were many students, especially girls, who were very upset.

One of the guidance counselors in my school was a pastor whose congregation could no longer afford to pay him. Ernie Herr was a special person. He continued with his church and went to work as a guidance counselor. The principal allowed Ernie and me to escort about twenty students to the funeral parlor that was only six blocks from the school. This was my first experience at a wake where the people screamed and carried on. One girl even fainted against me. She was still shaky on the way back to the school, and so I held onto her arm. This experience did do one very important thing for me. It brought home the reality that we are all one.

CRISIS TWO

I looked forward to going to work each day. It was never a boring job. Everything changed suddenly with the unfortunate incident of 1991. As I had said, Crown Heights and the Lubavitch Jewish Community were nearby. The lead car of the motorcade of Rabbi Schneerson, the community leader, as they were leaving the temple on Eastern Parkway, accidentally hit and killed a six-year-old young boy. The community was in an uproar because the Jewish ambulance that arrived on the scene went first to the driver of the car and took care of him while the boy lay in the street dying. Activist leaders riled the community. A gang murdered a Jewish student from Australia. Two days following the incident students returned to school. While most of the students were fine the gang members among them apparently thought that their activist leaders had given them permission to attack white people. During that year sixty-nine staff members were attacked in Wingate High School alone. Never was this reported in the newspapers. Never was it reported in any media. The principal, who was attacked with water balloons, resigned at the end of the year, and took a job in Long Island. In actuality they were not really water balloons. At that time the school was giving out condoms free to students. The students would fill them with water and throw them at staff and also at each other. This is how the government uses our money. I was opening my office in a side corridor of the second floor. All of a sudden I was hit in the back of my head harder than I was ever hit in my life. My face was smashed into the door. I took a second shot to the lower back. I had already had problems in both areas from childhood injuries spoken of earlier. Both injuries were exacerbated tremendously. When I turned around there were four male teenagers standing around me in a semi-circle. They called me a white Jew " B". Whenever there is action students come running. Within several seconds I was confronted by at least thirty students. They started to throw "water" balloons at me. For a few minutes we faced off. Eventually the school librarian, a lovely black woman, came out of her office. Once she arrived on the scene the students took off. The principal sent me home and told me to take some time off. I was at work the next day, but was never the same.

After the attack I would stay in my office, with the door locked when students were changing classes. If I happened to be in the hall and heard footsteps coming up behind me my hair would suddenly rise. This is a sign of over arousal of the sympathetic nervous system called piloerection. It is common in Post Traumatic Stress Disorder. The love I had for this job was lost, and I felt badly about it.

DISABILITY

Now, at this time, I was getting up at 4:45 in the morning. I worked as a school psychologist from seven a.m. until two-thirty p.m. I then grabbed a bite to eat and started my office hours from three p.m until eight p.m in Brooklyn. I reached home in New Jersey around nine-thirty, got to bed by ten-thirty and it started all over again. I even worked from eight a.m until six p.m on Saturdays. The combination of being attacked and injured and all the driving I was doing eventually took a toll. By the year after being attacked I was struggling to walk. Just getting out of the car was an extremely painful ordeal. The principal saw me struggling to walk one day and called me into his office. After we talked for a while, he said *"Dennis I don't want you killing yourself. I am sending you to the medical division to see about a medical sabbatical."* Before going I went to see an orthopedic doctor on my own. He ordered an MRI. They found three herniated disks and stenosis in my lower spine and two herniated disks in the neck. The doctor told me the lumbar disks were impinging on a nerve and I could be paralyzed if I didn't have an operation. He told me they would first try to shave the disks down to relieve the pain. If that didn't work they would have to consider fusing the disks. I didn't take this too well. I took his report to the Board of Education Medical Bureau. Its doctor examined me and reviewed the report. His decision was we couldn't offer you a medical sabbatical because the problem is severe and the chances of you ever returning to work are so small. He told me to apply for a disability retirement. It was impossible for me to even try to return to work as a school psychologist because of the severe pain, and work demands. At this time I had cut down my private office hours by bringing in another psychologist and a social worker to my office. I never wanted to be anyone's boss, and so just charged them rent for the space and referred patients to them. I filled out the application for the disability retirement, and made the appointment to be examined by the Retirement Board. This started something that changed my practice forever. The doctor who examined me saw me for no more than five minutes. He wrote a report saying that there was nothing at all wrong with me and I should return to work. I called the union. They told me that the Board of Education Medical Bureau would have to certify my return, and as it had evaluated me and denied my medical sabbatical they weren't going to go against what they had said. What an incredible situation to be in. I can't have a disability retirement, but I can't return to work. I found out that I could appeal the decision. The N.Y.C. Board of Health would send me out to see three doctors for what was called an "independent medical examination or IME." If two out of the three doctors ruled in my favor they had to grant the disability retirement. I once again filed paperwork and the procedure began. Three months later I was sent to the first doctor. This man didn't know me. He read my orthopedic doctor's report and examined me for less than five minutes. He said the Board of Health would get his report. A month later I saw the second doctor. He didn't want to see my doctor's report, but went on to question me for five minutes, and then examine me for no more than two minutes. After this I got really upset. I couldn't sleep the night before the final doctor's visit. These people didn't know me from Adam and yet were going to make a decision that could have major implications for my life. The final doctor had a plush office in upper Manhattan, and was the only one to spend a good fifteen minutes examining me. A few months later I got the decision in the mail. All three doctors found me totally disabled from ever working again as a school psychologist. I was on pins and needles because I was honest with each, and told them that I intended to continue working in private practice. The difference being that I could arrange my schedule to take multiple breaks to exercise and even stand during sessions if needed. I could also avoid rush hour traffic, and didn't have to drive as far. I worked three days a week the first two years. I would see two patients. Take a half-hour break to stretch and exercise, and see two more. Take a half-hour break and see the final two. The Board of Education had the right to reevaluate me after one year. Once again they sent me to their doctor who said there was nothing at all wrong with me. Once again I was forced to appeal the decision and go through the awful process again. Fortunately the doctors once again agreed that I was disabled and they had to continue the small pension they continue to give me. My concern was the medical coverage for my family.

I was constantly reading through the Internet for ways to get better. After failures with epidural shots in the spine, chiropractic and physical therapy, I hit on the treatment that literally saved my life-neuromuscular massage. Neuromuscular massage was not at all what I had expected it to be. The initial therapist was a Puerto Rican woman who turned out to be very strong. During our first session she warned me that this was going to hurt. She told me she would break up the spasms in my back, bring healing blood flow to the area, and desensitize me to pain. She turned out to be a godsend.

Twice weekly I was twisted like a pretzel, and then spent the rest of the hour with an elbow in my back digging into the painful spots. It hurt like hell, but I didn't care. I had a wife and three young children at home, and would do anything to get my life back on track. I remember going shopping to the mall with my wife and children. I struggled to walk in much pain but laughed the entire time. I never wanted my children to know how much I hurt. Once, a few years after beginning treatment, I travelled to a meeting in Boston. On the day I was set to return my back spasms were really bad after sitting for so long. On the way home I needed to cross Eighth Avenue to get to the train. I was taking baby steps and carrying my briefcase. It took me two lights to get across the street. This was Manhattan and so I have always wondered if the drivers thought this was a movie being shot. No cars beeped at me. After maybe six months of treatment with neuromuscular massage I found myself starting to walk a little better, and the severe pain wasn't as often. I don't want to be overly explicit, but anyone who has this problem knows the absolute torture of trying to have a bowel movement. Any relief is a blessing. After one year the therapist told me to start working out with lightweights to strengthen my upper body and back muscles. The goal she said was to take pressure off my lower back muscles. My orthopedic doctor had told me not to lift anything as it could paralyze me, but then his pills had only made me depressed. She was helping me, and I followed her advice. For some reason I had total faith that she would get me better. I now know how important faith is. The final section of this book will explain that. After two years the therapist and her husband moved to Florida. Fortunately, one of the other neuromuscular therapists in their office (Mark) took over my treatment. Mark Carangelo was every bit as good as my initial therapist. He was also a young man with dreams and motivation. He now has his own school of massage therapy in New Jersey, has worked for the New York Jets, and gives continuing education workshops around the country. I continue to see him weekly for treatment. Over time I did continue improving. As I got better I increased my office hours. I now begin every day with fifteen minutes of stretching. I then exercise at least one hour a day. I stretch again at night. Pain medication I take only at bedtime. I have tried sleeping without it but found myself tossing and turning for hours trying to get comfortable, and keeping my wife awake. Nighttime medication anaesthetizes me enough to rest a full night, and I wake up refreshed. In 2014 I suddenly had extreme pain in my neck. For four months I couldn't lie down with my head on a pillow. MRI's found severe arthritis and spurring that is inflaming matters. Instead of undergoing the shots that my pain management doctor offered my neuromuscular massage therapist and I developed a program to help the problem. So far it is working. I offer this insight so that others going through similar problems see that there is hope, and it comes mostly from inside you. Never give up hope, and never solely rely on one doctor's advice. I still have pain when sitting for a while and getting up or driving for more than a half-hour or sometimes just reaching for a towel but it is not to the point of disrupting my life any longer. It doesn't have to be that way for you either. The key is you're taking control of your treatment and not just sitting back and leaving it up to someone else to cure you. Remember no one is more concerned with you.

TREATING PATIENTS
WITH DISABILITIES

Going through this personal crisis in my life made me do a lot of thinking. If I struggled so greatly with disabling pain and a severely disrupted life I wondered how other people were coping with it. It was never a part of my practice before. It turns out that a neighbor was chief judge of the Brooklyn Workers' Compensation Board. We discussed things when we met at our pool club. Water happens to be great therapy for sore muscles. It turned out that licensed psychologists had only recently been authorized by the New York State Workers' Compensation Board to treat patients. Up until then only psychiatrists could treat injured workers. I immediately applied and was accepted. I believe that I may have been the first psychologist in Brooklyn to be authorized to treat patients by the WCB. It turned out to be an incredible experience, and a passion that altered my practice forever. My specialty became treating patients suffering emotional problems that were secondary to disabling physical injuries and a severely disrupted life. One of my first patients I still stay in touch with. He was performing electrical work on the ceiling of a warehouse approximately twenty feet above the ground. The type of bucket lift you see from the electrical company lifted him there. Unfortunately, the operator of the lift hit the wrong button and the bucket turned over. My patient fell to the floor. He was rushed to the hospital. It was touch and go but he survived. He had landed on his back, and suffered extensive orthopedic damage. Try to imagine for a moment this was you. You wake up in a hospital in serious pain, and are told that your disabilities are such that you will probably never be able to work again. Your first thoughts are but I have a wife and young child. I have a house, a mortgage, and car payments. How will I be able to support them? Your fear is tremendous. Within one year my patients wife had left him because he was no longer "a man." These are the types of patients I began treating. It certainly wasn't what I was trained for in school or even in my postgraduate psychotherapy training. I did have one thing going for me that was critical though. I had been there, and I understood. I even kept a copy of my MRI's in the office, showing five badly herniated disks, just in case a patient was skeptical. Most doctors and ancillary personnel treating my patients lacked this understanding because they hadn't lived it themselves. Patients constantly complained to me that their doctors or other therapists just don't understand.

In order to help patients there was so much to learn. First, came the system. Never in my life was I confronted by such a dysfunctional system. Patients had to prove in Workers' Compensation court that they had a work related disability before any diagnostic tests, surgery, or treatment would be covered by insurance and performed. To complicate matters hearings were scheduled approximately six months apart, and at each hearing only one issue was dealt with. This was the case because lawyers would take on a huge load of cases and give little time to each person. They were constantly, like rats, scampering from case to case. I use this analogy because very few of them showed compassion or even interest in the patients. Almost everyone would complain that they never returned phone calls.

Psychiatrists are medical doctors and they proved to be problematic for me. Before insurance companies would pay for psychotherapy they had the right to send the patient out to a psychiatrist for an independent medical examination. In the early years of my specialty the IME psychiatrists almost always denied the need for psychotherapy. At the next hearing a trial would be set to see "who is truthful." Over the years I have been involved in more than one hundred such trials. Never have I lost one. The reason is obvious. IME psychiatrists see a patient once for fifteen minutes on average. I have been seeing the patient once weekly for forty-five minutes, and I usually involve the spouse in sessions soon after we begin treatment. Not only the patients, but also the whole family's life has been disrupted. I learned this with my first disabled patient. I won every case because I knew the patient infinitely better and could describe in detail how his or her life was so changed and led directly to his or her anxiety and depressive symptoms. Six months following the trial the court would rule in my favor and authorize treatment. For me what this would mean is that I would have to wait about two years before getting paid, but then I would receive all back monies owed. Because of this time lag very, very few psychologists would treat patients. It meant for me that I only accepted patients from a few medical doctors I got to know well, and carefully reviewed their medical findings. I wanted to be sure that the injuries were real, and I could then argue in court that emotional problems developed secondarily to the life disruption that they caused. Twice lawyers had tried to refer patients to me. I quickly realized they were not truly disabled. The lawyers were trying to build a case. For example, one person was a maintenance worker in a homeless shelter. Supposedly a big black man asked him for a cigarette and when he refused him the black man punched the white maintenance worker in the face. "He *is traumatized and cannot go near black people was the lawyers argument."* I had developed a positive reputation in the courts and wouldn't touch this with a ten-foot pole. Not even a twenty-foot pole. The second person referred was a 21- year old young man. He had fallen at work and was found to have one bulging disk in his lumbar spine. When I interviewed him he told me "*I hate working and need you to help get me out of it. I never want to work again."* I told him his case was a difficult one to prove and he would need the very best to represent him. I referred him to a psychiatrist that I really didn't like because his ego was so big, and he had treated one of my patients rudely and upset her because she had the nerve to question him.

The one exception to the normal procedure was patients injured on 9-11. In that case insurance companies waived the requirements and actually called me to treat patients. This was the only time that requirements were waived. No one could deny the Post Traumatic Stress Disorder that these people suffered. I have found that some people are not aware of the severity of the 9-11 attack for those who lived but became disabled. One example should change all that. I will call her Joan. Joan was working for a company on the 105th floor of building two of the World Trade Center. When the first building was hit she and her coworkers became upset. Reportedly, the supervisors told everyone to stay calm. It was just a plane accident and wouldn't affect them. As time went by and news spread Joan and her coworkers ignored the request to stay at their desks. They began walking down the stairwell. Joan told me that she was around the 60th floor when her building was hit. *"I was thrown down a flight of stairs and people banged into me."* Joan walked the remaining 60 floors in darkness and toxic smoke. Her friend stopped to help a woman who was frozen by panic. The friend didn't make it out. Joan made it, but suffered significant orthopedic damage from being thrown down a flight of steps. She was taken to the hospital, and eventually saw private doctors for treatment.

A few years later she began having breathing problems. Lung damage was found. Over the next several years the lung damage worsened. She is now awaiting a lung transplant, and relies on oxygen to help her breathe. Imagine what she is going through, and then know that she had three young children, and was the main financial support in the home. While Joan's case was the worst of those from 9-11 I had treated she was not the only one. I saw patients who would jump out of bed when a fire engine or other loud noise startled them. I treated one woman who was lucky enough to escape the building but then was knocked unconscious and broke her ankle when the fleeing crowd trampled her. Fortunately a passerby carried her to the safety of a storefront. She awoke covered in cement dust and also developed breathing problems. Among survivors nightmares, startle reactions, fears for personal safety etc. are common. PTSD fears may lessen over time, but will never go away totally.

As upsetting as the day of infamy was the sick system only compounded matters. Most medical doctors in the Workers' Compensation system would wait for treatment authorization before performing any needed surgeries. I remember the patient with a broken hand who waited two years to get surgery. She eventually developed a severe pain disorder called RSD or reflex sympathetic dystrophy. To understand the severity of this think of a bad cut you once had. Initially there is pain. Once the healing occurs the pain stops. With RSD, for some reason, the pain never stops but worsens and can spread throughout the whole body. Her doctor blamed this on the fact that she had to wait so long for treatment. I wish this was unusual, but it wasn't. Many patients would have to wait at least one year just to get an MRI.

The reason the system is so dysfunctional is that it is arranged as an adversarial system where the insurance company tries to limit its losses, and personal lawyers argue to get the highest possible payments for patients because their fee is related to it. I think the picture is pretty clear. Doctor's who perform IME's for the insurance company know that if they write good reports for the patient the insurance company will put them on the bottom of their referral list. Their income will thus suffer. There was one doctor that I have called the million-dollar man. I call him this because he admitted in court that on the prior year he had earned one million dollars solely from his work for insurance companies. Most of this money came from third party lawsuits. For example, one patient of mine was cutting up the streets of Manhattan for the installation of Verizon FIOS. He was doing this using a wet saw. He hit a Con Edison feeder box that was supposed to be, but wasn't, lower in the ground and protected by a steel plate. He ended up suffering a heart attack and also received multiple neurological and orthopedic injuries. Such an injury was not the fault of his work but that of a third party. Therefore he could sue. The doctor in question always wrote long horrible reports about such patients. He always said that they were malingers, and then charged at least twenty thousand dollars to represent the insurance company in court. There are doctors out there who have literally sold their soul to the devil for money. The system is not at all designed with the best interests of patients at heart. Rather, it frustrates patients incredibly, makes their physical problems worse by denying timely treatment, and makes their emotional problems much worse and much more difficult to treat. I will drive the dysfunction of the system home with my most upsetting case. It was the woman mentioned earlier with a broken hand.

Mrs. H was a bright, highly motivated woman. While working as a department manager for a telecommunications concern in Manhattan she was injured. The injury occurred when she was leaving a manager's meeting. The floor outside the meeting room had been washed during the meeting, but no wet floor sign was placed to warn them. Mrs. H took a nasty fall, and broke three bones in her left wrist. She applied for Workers' Compensation. At the first hearing, months after her fall, the insurance company argued that there was no proof that the injury had occurred at work. The judge ordered Mrs. H to obtain proof. At the next hearing months later she provided affidavits from coworkers. Before allowing surgery the insurance company sent Mrs. H for an independent medical examination. The doctor who performed the independent medical examination denied the need for surgery. A trial was set. Months later her own doctor and the insurance companies doctor testified. Months later the judge ruled for her doctor. Two years following the injury Mrs. H had her left hand operated on. If you are wondering why she didn't pay for the operation on her own know that her husband was deceased and she was the sole support for her two daughters and her son. The pain, instead of subsiding, worsened. Six months later a pain management doctor diagnosed Reflex Sympathetic Dystrophy. He told her the length of time she was forced to wait for the operation was the probable cause. By the time she was referred to me she was severely depressed and so incredibly frustrated. I referred her to a psychiatrist for medication as an adjunct to psychotherapy. As time progressed her Reflex Sympathetic Dystrophy (RSD) continued to spread throughout her body. I learned from the internet and also the pharmacological training that I was participating in at the time just how devastating this disease is. Basically your nervous system is progressively being destroyed. While the cause is still not fully understood RSD can develop from relatively minor bruising or operations. Eventually a spinal cord stimulator was implanted to help relieve some of the pain she was in. The concept is simple. Pain signals travel upwards to the brain where they are interpreted. The Spinal Cord Stimulator sends an impulse down to block some of the pain signal. In theory this can prove helpful. As time went by a second spinal cord stimulator was implanted for greater coverage of her body. Next a paddle lead was added to the first stimulator. When we last spoke Mrs. H spent much of her day in a wheelchair, and she is awaiting a morphine pump be implanted. To make matters even worse the insurance company recently put a new examiner on her case. The new examiner is denying her medical transportation and sending her out, once again, for independent medical examinations.

This bright, highly motivated woman's life was destroyed by a dysfunctional system. The insurance company could have saved a huge amount of money if they had only allowed the operation right away. Such is the system.

As I have already mentioned working with individuals suffering emotional problems secondary to disabling physical disabilities is not at all what I was trained to do in psychotherapy. I knew I would have to retrain. These patients were suffering, and I wanted to help them the best I could. It became the majority of my practice, and since most psychologists avoided this specialty I have included in appendix 1 guidelines for mental health practitioners who wish to work with this severely underserved population.

TRAINING IN
PSYCHOPHARMACOLOGY

All of my patients were taking multiple medications, and since I was the person who best knew each person, I felt it my responsibility to better understand medication interactions and side effects. It so happens that just before I had started this new specialty the Department of Defense had started a demonstration project. Military psychologists were trained in a two-year program at the army physician assistant training school to prescribe psychoactive medications. Upon completion of the training program they then underwent a period of supervision by medical doctors. The program, an each psychologist, was closely monitored by the American Medical Association for obvious reasons. The AMA has fought against dentists, podiatrists and any other group they see as a threat to its monopoly over healthcare. They have tried everything possible to block competing professions. Ten psychologists completed the program and began prescribing. The program itself was evaluated as being highly successful, but "due to financial considerations was terminated." I later learned all about politics and lobbying in making such decisions. The trained prescribing psychologists were assigned patients from the same pool as were military psychiatrists. What was found was exactly what I had expected. The psychologists prescribed medication to less than twenty percent of the patients. The psychiatrists prescribed medication to almost one hundred percent of the patients. Additionally psychologists tended to prescribe fewer medications, and for shorter periods of time. Why the discrepancy? Psychiatrists have but one tool to treat patients. Psychologists, on the other hand, have multiple tools, and while pills do have their place in treatment, I have never seen the pill that can teach a patient how to cope with problems of living. Although I could offer numerous examples of the fallacy of prescribing medication for many emotional problems there is one that stands out. A very depressed young woman had been referred to my practice by one of her friends. I will call her Samantha. During the initial interview I had found out that Samantha had dated her boyfriend since high school, and now that they had both graduated college they set their wedding date. Two weeks prior to the wedding she came home to find a message on her answering machine. He was calling off the wedding. No explanation was given. She tried calling him to no avail. She later found out that he had been cheating on her for years. Try to imagine yourself in this situation for a minute. You had dated someone for many years and were deeply in love. In your mind were dreams of a happy future, and then one message turned your world upside down. Samantha was distraught. She couldn't eat. She couldn't sleep. Panic attacks were constant. Her parents took her to a psychiatrist who prescribed an antidepressant and a sleep aid. Her symptoms worsened. Samantha was losing weight. She still wasn't sleeping more than a few hours and it wasn't restful sleep. Fortunately a friend suggested she see me. Psychotherapy takes time, but it is a human relationship, and in times like she was facing human compassion was what she needed rather than a pill. The first few sessions I let her vent and tried to teach her deep relaxation with guided imagery to help her rest more peacefully. Once we had developed a positive therapeutic relationship I told her "You are a beautiful and very special young woman and I am so happy that you found out now what kind of person he was. Imagine if you had married and had children and then he did a disappearing act from your life." This struck a chord in her. I kept on this theme until she accepted it fully and she said *"I will prove to him what he missed out on."* Instead of feeling sorry for herself she threw herself into her work as a kindergarten teacher, and went back to school. With this regaining of the control in her life her depression disappeared. When I last saw her she was engaged to a nice young man, and was working on her doctorate. This is but one case. Every psychologist out there could tell you of multiple cases like this. Psychiatrists however will keep prescribing their pills. In many cases all they are doing is hindering people from getting the help that they need, and making people even more depressed and without hope.

Shortly after the Department of Defense initiated its program an entrepreneurial psychologist, Dr. Sam Feldman, decided that medication prescribing psychologists would be a boon to society. Patients would no longer have to see two doctors to be treated for emotional problems. It would save patients, and society, money as well as time and also would lead to more integrated care. This last would be the case, because from my own experience, the communication between psychologists and psychiatrists leaves a lot to be desired. It is much better that one person treat both aspects of the patient. As an aside, Up until the 1970's medical students desiring to become psychiatrists were required to undergo training in counseling and psychotherapy during their psychiatric residency. These are the psychiatrists that you may have seen in the movies. During the 1970's the American Psychiatric Association made the decision to restrict training of future psychiatrists solely to diagnosis of problems and prescribing medication. A definite part of this decision was the fact that psychiatrists were, at that time, the least well paid, and least well respected of any medical doctors. Today this is no longer the case. Psychiatrists who restrict their practices to prescribing medications solely are now a well-paid profession. Respect is another matter.

Back to Sam Feldman and the training of psychologists. Sam took it on himself to design and implement a training program, similar to the one established by the Department of Defense, for private practicing psychologists. The program he named "The Prescribing Psychologists' Register." Classes were held both in New York and

California. Approximately five hundred psychologists enrolled in both states. I immediately enrolled. The training turned out to be some of the most challenging I have encountered, but also the most rewarding. Unquestionably it made me a better psychologist. Workshops were held once monthly on weekends in hotels. Prior to attending a workshop each enrollee was given a stack of material to read and memorize. Doctors of pharmacology led the first seven workshops. At the end of each eighteen-hour workshop we were required to pass a one hundred question test, which incorporated material both from the readings and the workshop. Once passed you could then move on to the next workshop. Workshops number eight and on were led by a medical doctor in a specialty area. Once again we were given readings prior to attending the workshop. All told I completed almost four hundred and fifty hours of training in psychopharmacology and related medical sciences. The training opened my eyes to the magnificence of the human body, and has made me a much better psychologist. I now understood fully the reasons for drug interactions and drug side effects. I even had knowledge that some medical doctors weren't aware of. For example I was aware of the pain disorder RSD ten years prior to some of the medical doctors I consulted with.

Those psychologists who wished to eventually be able to prescribe medication were also required to undergo a one year supervised preceptorship by a medical doctor. Today the training is being done at universities. A Master's degree in clinical psychopharmacology is being awarded to psychologists who complete the programs. Unfortunately, regardless of the mounting evidence proving the safety of trained prescribing psychologists, few states have authorized psychologists to prescribe to date. The reason is obvious to anyone who understands the political process. State legislatures are required to vote to change the laws allowing psychologists to prescribe, and legislators, as a rule, are more interested in money for their reelection coffers than they are for the welfare of the public. This has become a nightmare of a problem for politics in the United States. If only our leaders would do the right thing for society rather than for themselves. What we need badly in this country are statesmen and not politicians. Statesmen are busy professionals who take time out from their careers to serve the public interests for a few years. Politicians are another matter and spend their time looking for ways to get re-elected. They, not all, vote more with their pocketbook then the welfare of society in mind. Term limits for all politicians is a must if we are ever going to change this. Even more important is to change political financing laws. Public financing of elections will level the playing field. Television stations and news outlets must donate time and space to all candidates equally. Only then will we have the democracy that we truly yearn for. The election of 2016 is evidence of how angry the public is getting towards politicians.

Treating patients suffering emotional problems secondary to disabling physical injuries became my specialty for the last twenty years of my practice. Treating disabled people whose life was absolutely devastated meant so much to me. I learned so much about their needs, and how to best treat them. As a side benefit helping patients cope with their problems actually helped me deal with mine.

CRISIS 3

It was a June day in 2008. My wife, a substitute teacher, and myself were both off that day. At eight a.m. my wife got out of bed. I was feeling lazy and said I would rest a few more minutes. Ten minutes later I threw off my covers and stood up. Immediately I collapsed. My initial thought was that I had stood up too quickly, and the blood didn't have a chance to reach my brain yet. This condition is called orthostatic hypotension, and is found to be a problem with a number of medications. I pulled myself back onto the bed. The second time I stood up more slowly. Once again I immediately collapsed. Now I began to worry. Being stubborn I once again pulled myself up on to the bed and tried once more to stand up. This time when I collapsed I was really scared. I tried calling to my wife for help. After two minutes she came into the room and said, *"what are you squawking about?"* It appears that what I thought I was calling out turned out to be unintelligible. My wife took one look at the fear on my face and started yelling for my children to get up quickly. Both my son and one of my daughters were EMT's on the township first aid squad. They took one look at me and ran to the phone. The first aid squad arrived in less than fifteen minutes. The captain of the squad said *"don't worry we take care of our own."* They rushed me to the hospital, and called ahead so that they would be prepared for me. During the ride there I laid on a stretcher trying to block out the voice of the young female EMT riding in the back with me so that I could do arithmetic in my mind. I kept praying that it still worked. When I got to the hospital I was rushed straight through the emergency room and into a treatment room. There a nurse was waiting to hook me up to Heparin, a blood thinner. Fortunately the stroke was mild. By nighttime I was beginning to speak intelligibly, and the next day I could walk unaided. By the third day I would walk the halls, holding my IV pole in one hand, for an hour by day and an hour by night. The nurses kidded my wife that they had me under surveillance should I try to escape. On the fourth day they found, what they believe was the cause of the stroke. Some plaque appeared to have broken off from my ascending aorta and went to the brain where it broke a small vessel. They had found the bleed.

Once they believed they had found the reason for the stroke I was released and sent home under my wife's eye. On the fourth day at home I could not stand it anymore and told my wife I was going to work. The car trip I will never forget. I was driving on the highways doing almost seventy when traffic started getting heavy. All of a sudden I remembered my doctor telling me that I could have another stroke at any time. As I thought this and realized that I could hit and maybe kill someone at the speed we were travelling my heart started racing and my breathing was coming fast. I recognized the onset of a panic attack and immediately went into action. Through the years I had taught enough patients how to minimize panic attacks, and now that training would come in handy. I purposefully slowed my breathing. I thought to myself that having a panic attack is stupid, and only will increase the likelihood of my having an accident. I then turned on the radio to a music channel, and concentrated on the words of the songs. This was a way of distracting myself. Within a few minutes the panic attack was over and never occurred again. Understand that it took me years to learn how to do this, and you must believe it will work.

I did have symptoms from my stroke but they didn't stop me from working. What they did do was annoy me. For years I have played stickball every Sunday morning during the summer. That summer I struck out almost every time I was up, and was terrible at fielding.

My coordination and reflexes were off, and still are a bit of a problem even today. Further when I was speaking to patients once in a while I would mean to say one thing but another word would come out. This is a symptom of aphasia caused by the stroke. Fortunately it didn't happen often and I would just laugh when it did. Luckily for me most of my patients by this point in time were disabled and were understanding and even encouraging.

Thankfully I am a psychologist and had learned that the best way to overcome symptoms of a stroke is to be proactive. The book "The Brain that Changes Itself" is remarkable. Imagine a college teacher who suffered stroke damage to ninety percent of his brain, and in one year he is back to teaching. His adult children refused to help him with tasks that he struggled with. They also tied down his good arm, and made him utilize his weakened one. In addition to retraining damaged body parts passionately learning something new helps create new neural nets. I worked on both techniques. For purposes of this book I will focus on the educational technique. As I had never studied physics in either high school or college I began reading everything I could get my hands on. I began with studying Tycho Brahe and Johannes Kepler in the sixteenth century and worked my way through Newton, Bohr, Einstein, Feynman, etc. all the way up to the very latest theoretical physics and cosmology. While I was doing this to help me overcome the stroke symptoms I was not prepared for the change it would bring about to my life.

Physics led me directly to a study of paranormal phenomena and that into a study of consciousness and prayer. This section of the book will be the largest and aspects of it are difficult for a layman, even a professional, to understand.. Thus I will proceed slowly and attempt to build a strong case for how science supports spirituality.

Many of my colleagues doubt the existence of a creator because they believe that science has brought doubt on religious teachings. The point I wish to emphasize is that it was science that led me directly to a study of paranormal behaviors and spirituality. It was science that led me to a creator.

THE GROWTH OF SCIENCE

As mentioned, to help my recovery from the stroke I began reading everything I could relating to physics and cosmology. The first book I read was titled "Tycho and Kepler" by Kitty Fergusen. Just as when I first began college thirty-five years earlier I was like a human sponge. I was enthralled by the intense desire these people had for better understanding the universe we inhabit, and also by the many obstacles they faced. For me learning about the times they lived in and the lifestyles they lived was enjoyable and eye opening. Although it had nothing to do with his science but finding out how Tycho Brahe died both shocked me and also showed me how much we have changed for better and for worse. The story of his death was so shocking that I will begin with it. On October 13, 1601, Tycho was invited to a dinner at a noblemen's house. While at the dinner table he had to urinate badly. At that time, it was considered the height of bad manners to leave the table until the head of the household had done so first. Tycho was first and foremost a gentleman of the times and so he held it in. By the time he returned home, he could not urinate anymore. Tycho tried everything but to no avail. After several days had gone by he began suffering intestinal fever and eventually became delirious. On October 24th he passed away. This story clearly showed the incredible value that seventeenth century noblemen placed on proper etiquette. Tycho endangered his life rather than allowing himself to be seen as a bad guest. The very next book I read was about the life of Niels Bohr, another nobleman. Bohr manifested similar qualities of etiquette and respect. Not only was I impressed by the sense of respect that was exhibited but I was also fascinated by both their lifestyles. Noblemen interested in the sciences would bring apprentices into their compounds and spend their days designing studies. Then at night they would sit around sampling brandy and thoroughly debate the day's scientific results. When I think of all the stress we live under in the twenty-first century and how alienated people have become this look into the past was refreshing. Imagine that just sixty years ago people wore suits to baseball games. While there are both positives and negatives to the change in people in my eyes the greatest negative is in the decline in respect for one's fellow man.

Getting back to science, Tycho was a nobleman and so had the financial resources to pursue his interests. He spent the greater part of his life trying to understand the workings of the universe. There were no telescopes for him to use. Instead he had scientific equipment made to order, and he kept extremely detailed records of his observations of the universe. When we say universe what we are really talking about was the Milky Way Galaxy since this was the brightest and best seen part of the universe visible to the naked eye. Tycho was apparently very secretive and kept his records to himself. As he got older he took on an apprentice who was from a poor family and did not have the financial resources that Tycho Brahe had to pursue his passion. Johannes Kepler may not have been wealthy but he was a very bright mathematician. Following Tycho's death Kepler gained access to the full thirty-five years of recorded observations that Tycho had made. Kepler went through the information and came up with startling discoveries. He provided the mathematics that strengthened the Copernican model of the universe. Kepler also helped us understand the elliptical orbits of planets, and this was done without the aid of telescopes. Fortunately for him he did so in a Lutheran country. The Roman Catholic Church was not yet ready to give up its cosmology and the dogma tied to it. In Copernicus' time the Roman Catholic Church was so powerful. It had developed a dogma to explain all of creation and God's will. Unfortunately, as with any bureaucracy power tends to corrupt, and corrupt it did. Anyone daring to question church teachings was subject to torture and even death. The inquisition was brutal. Fortunately, Copernicus was nobody's fool. He had seen a fellow scientist (Bruno) burned at the stake for speaking out about Copernican theories of a sun centered solar system. Copernicus waited until he was near death to publish his theories in a book. The church had held science back but it could not stop it completely. There will always be inquisitive minds that will not be quieted.

By the seventeenth century philosophers such as Bacon, Hobbes, Descartes and others had begun the change of worldview. Instead of a focus on religion they saw the world from a deterministic worldview. The world and everything in it was created from atoms, and followed mechanistic laws. The universe was like a giant watch and God was the watchmaker. If you knew where a particle was and it's velocity you could predict where it would be at any time in the future. As consciousness could not be tested directly it was pushed to the side. The body was the realm of science. Consciousness was the realm of religion.

By the mid seventeenth century science was on the move. What I believe was the greatest of all scientific achievements and the one thing that led to the immense progress in science was the formalization of the scientific method. Utilizing the scientific method scientists would make observations of some behavior whether it would be the movements of planets, accelerating mass or an illness. These scientists would then develop hypotheses to try to understand their observations. Next they developed predictions based on their hypotheses. Tests would then be carried out to test the predictions. If a hypothesis was accepted by the initial test it would then be repeated. Once enough tests were performed that confirmed the hypothesis it would be accepted as an explanation of some behavior. For example, Ignaz Semmelweiss, a Hungarian medical doctor, noticed that when interns delivered babies there was a much higher mortality rate than when midwives delivered babies. Ignaz did some detective work and found that the interns began their day working on cadavers. Ignaz postulated that something he called germs were responsible for the greater mortality. He demanded that the interns wash their hands thoroughly before delivering babies.

The medical community fought him because "germs" could not be seen.

Ignaz stuck to his guns, *and voila not so many deaths.* This story makes a point pretty clearly. It is always a difficult struggle to change a prevailing paradigm in thinking. We are seeing this today with the new scientific paradigm. The reductionistic and materialistic thinking of the last three hundred years is so deeply ingrained in society that there are people who are fighting change.

The important point regarding the scientific method is that if even one test did not confirm findings it would lead scientists to revise their theories in an attempt to more fully explain them.

A good example is Newton's laws. For three hundred years Newton's Laws of Motion were accepted and these laws still are used to explain such things as the trajectory of spaceships. Einstein came along and developed the theory of relativity, which was an improved theory of the universe. Newton thought gravity was an inherent feature of the mass of an object. Einstein showed that gravity is the result of the geometry of the universe. Even further, Newton's laws were materialistic laws. If you knew the starting point of a particle and the velocity of that particle one could predict exactly where the particle would be at any given time. Along comes Niels Bohr and the Copenhagen school of quantum mechanics. One of the young apprentices of Dr. Bohr, Werner Heisenberg, proved that it is impossible to know the velocity and position of a particle at the same time, as observation of one would effect the measurement of the other. Heisenberg's "uncertainty principle" has so far stood the passage and test of time. Actually quantum mechanics showed that Newton's laws do not hold for the world of the ultra small, but only for large bodies, and therefore cannot be complete explanations. Little by little science builds on earlier findings. The greatest example of this is Einstein. At the beginning of the twentieth century Einstein took a big pot. In the pot he threw in the mathematical equations of Maxwell. Next he inserted the non-linear geometry of Riemann. Finally, Einstein seasoned the pot with some of his own thought experiments. His creation earned him a spot on the Food Network with his "Theories of Relativity."

Today we are in the midst of another revolution in science. This one is the quantum revolution. The scientific study that began us looking differently at the world was a simple, but such an important study. Today it can be repeated in elementary and middle schools throughout the world to make an important point about reality.

In 1803 Dr. Thomas Young designed a study to evaluate the particle nature of light. Dr. Young coated one glass window with an opaque substance that allowed but a tiny pinpoint of light to enter. Behind the opening he apparently had something like an index card to split the light beam into two. Behind this he had a collecting screen to intercept the light beams. Now Young fully expected to find two darkened points of light on the screen when he came back from lunch. This would have confirmed his prediction that light consisted of point particles, but he got a big surprise. This surprise led to a lot of scientists scratching their heads, and would lead to much scientific investigation.

When Thomas Young came back from lunch what he found was not two darkened points of light, but instead bands of light and dark light. To understand what he had found think of the following scenario. Two speedboats are traveling parallel to each other and a distance apart. Each boat makes waves. When the waves meet at their high points you have Youngs' dark lines. When the waves meet at opposite points they cancel each other out and you have light lines. What Dr. Young had found was that points of light are actually waves. By today we have studied pretty much every particle found in nature. They all have the characteristic of being waves. The whole story is actually mind-boggling and makes us question our very concept of reality. It has been found that when we observe particles entering some form of test apparatus they appear as point particles, but when we go out to lunch, or figure out some sneaky way of observing the particles, we find that the particles have a wave nature. The thing that determines whether we find a wave or a point is **our observation**. We are the ones to determine the reality we see. This type of study has been repeated literally thousands of times and with all sorts of test apparatus and the findings are always the same. All particles found on earth and in cosmic rays have this dual nature.

By the 1800s science was picking up steam. Watt developed an improved version of the steam engine. Fulton designed the steamboat. Stephenson invented the steam locomotive. Goods got to market sooner, and people became more mobile. Whitney developed the cotton gin, which made manufacturing more economical. Assembly lines, sewing machines, improvements in transportation etc. all increased productivity and began to make society more materialistic. The industrial revolution was in full swing. Today we are experiencing the downside of materialistic thinking.

Science continued to make progress. By the 1800s Tyndall demonstrated the principle of fiber optics. Bell showed that voice could be transmitted on a beam of light. Faraday, a genius, but with little formal education, established the basis for the electromagnetic field in physics. Maxwell took Faraday's work further and summarized it in a set of equations that remains the basis of all modern theories of electromagnetic phenomena. The concept of energy fields has now been expanded to include the belief that all particles have their own energy field. Interacting energy fields throughout space has been a major breakthrough in our understanding of the universe and of so much more to be discussed.

By the end of the 1800s the technology had developed so that scientists like Curie, Thompson, Planck and Bohr could begin investigating aspects of the atom itself. Atoms had been postulated by the Greeks 2,000 years ago but we never before had the technology to actually see them. Technology was still minimal for the task but the experiments devised were absolutely brilliant. They were both physical and mental experiments. Einstein was a master of the latter. I have already shown how he would combine earlier findings and come up with an entirely new way of looking at them and then design a thought experiment to evaluate them. Interestingly he accomplished much of his earlier discoveries while at work in a patent office. A lesson to be learned by all; time should not be wasted. Einstein found that the one constant in the universe was the speed of light. All else is relative. Time, Einstein found, actually stops at the speed of light. Imagine this for a minute. Photons created in the big bang have been zipping around the universe since they were first created at the speed of light. Thus in terms of twenty-four hour earth bound days they have not aged. Time is meaningless for them. Physicist Gerald Schroeder uses this to give a whole new way of understanding the Bible and the age of the universe. More will be discussed of Schroeder in a bit. Unlike Newton, Einstein interpreted gravity as the warping of space by large objects such as suns and black holes. Einstein changed the world with his famous formula equating energy and mass $E=MC^2$. With this formula he showed us that what we consider mass is simply densely compacted energy, and now we know what happens when it is suddenly released.

The world had changed, and was soon about to get much stranger. Danish physicist Niels Bohr gained fame for his studies of the structure of the atom. He showed that electrons revolve around the nucleus of an atom in distinct energy levels. Only certain energy levels are allowed. When an electron moves from one level to a lower one energy is released. So far as I am concerned Bohr's greatest accomplishment was building the Copenhagen School of Physics. Bohr brought together the youngest and brightest physicist of his day to work on the new idea of quantum physics. What exactly is quantum physics? The idea is recognized as having started with physicist Max Planck. Around the year 1900 Planck was working on understanding the results obtained from "black bodies." A black body is a surface that absorbs all frequencies of light that hit it. The results could not be explained using Newtonian classical physics. Planck eventually developed an equation and a theory to explain the findings. The amazing thing about his new theory is that energy is actually discharged in small packets or quanta. Bohr's school of physics showed that when electrons jump from one energy level to another it is not in a smooth, continuous fashion but in a sudden "quantum leap." Think of all the television shows, movies and books that have used this term. Quantum mechanics was born and would change the world in ways that are simply astonishing.

By this point in time scientists now had the technological equipment, though still modest by today's standards, to visualize particles as they moved through cloud chambers and eventually particle accelerators. What scientists found is that all particles obey none of the laws of classical physics. For example all particles exist as waves until they are observed. Once the particles are "**aware**" of being observed they change their reality to become point particles. Well over one hundred particles have been found in particle accelerators and cosmic rays. They all manifest this finding. Particles that are so small you need electron microscopes to see them seem to exhibit some form of "awareness." Bohr's Copenhagen School went on to make a number of spectacular findings. Besides Heisenberg's "uncertainty principle," Schroedinger gave us the mathematical formulas for determining the wave function of a particle. What this means is that all particles exist only as statistical probabilities until they are observed. Once the particle is observed the wave function collapses and one probability becomes realized. As everything in existence is made up from these particles imagine what this says about "reality." Interestingly, in the 1950's physicist Hugh Everett took Schroedinger's findings literally and developed the "Many World's Hypothesis." This was one of the first theories of the multiverse.

Basically what Everett had hypothesized is that a universe must exist for every one of the quantum probabilities. In other words the wave function never collapses to only one reality. I can't even fathom this idea of Everett's. Every time you make a decision between two things a separate universe splits off. What I do accept, however, is that my three-dimensional mind is limited, and therefore may not be able to consider alternatives that could exist.

Another of Bohr's associates Wolfgang Pauli hypothesized the existence of the anti-electron or positron years before it was ever discovered and demonstrated. Mathematics told him the positron must exist. Today we know that every particle found has an anti-particle. When the two come together they annihilate each other. Author Dan Brown made use of antimatter in his book *"Angels and Demons."* I mention Pauli last for a reason. Pauli was undoubtedly one of the very brightest scientists of his day. He began working with psychologist, Carl Jung. Jung, after extensive travel and research into different cultures, had developed the theory of "universal archetypes." Jung developed this theory after noting that cultures, which had never come into contact, shared many similarities in beliefs and even architecture. Pauli agreed with Jung that there was some sort of universal informational field that all of us share in. According to both, consciousness could not be ruled out of science as we had done for three centuries. The concept of informational fields was to become one of the hottest topics in twenty-first century physics, and also the new field of quantum biology.

Relativity theory and quantum mechanics had opened a Pandora's box. Interestingly in the years prior to Einstein and Bohr there were several prominent physicists who remarked that physics was just about complete. All that remained to be done was dot a few I's and cross a few T's. The absolute gall of man to think we know more than a tiny fraction of all knowledge.

COSMOLOGICAL SURPRISES

At the same time that relativity theory and quantum mechanics were beginning to change everything we thought we knew about physics, and about reality, another theory was being shattered. For centuries men had believed the universe to be eternal and static. To show how deeply embedded this belief was no less a man than Albert Einstein altered his equations to add a constant term so that the universe would become static or unchanging. His original equations of the universe did not offer a static universe but Einstein, as many notable scientists, believed deeply in God, and felt that God would not "Play dice with his universe." In later years he would admit his mistake but, as often happens in science, this "mistake" years later turned up again to help explain more recent theories.

It was astronomer Edwin Hubble who shattered belief in a static universe. Prior to Hubble's findings it was thought that the Milky Way Galaxy was the entirety of the universe. Hubble, in the 1920's, was able to show two things that changed the way cosmology has been viewed since. First, was his finding that faint nebulae were in actuality distant galaxies. The Milky Way was not at all the entirety of the universe. Today, with our satellites and space telescopes we have identified hundreds of billions of galaxies. Most of these contain hundreds of billions of stars. Additionally, we are beginning to find that many of these stars have solar systems circling them. What are the odds that we are alone?

The second of his findings was that distant galaxies appear to be moving away from the Milky Way at an increasing speed. It was this finding that proved the fact that the universe was expanding. The easiest way for me to explain this last finding is this: If a car is moving towards you at high speed light waves are compressed or "blue shifted." If a car is moving away from you at high speed light waves are stretched or "red shifted." Hubble had found that the light from distant galaxies was red shifted. Cosmologists report that in a billion years or so all galaxies but our own will be beyond our horizon.

As a result of his findings, Edwin Hubble not only had a space telescope named after him, but he is considered by many to be responsible for the growth of the field of cosmology. Cosmologists today have come an incredibly long way in our understanding of the universe we live in, but there remain many unanswered questions.

One huge question to be answered was if the universe consists almost entirely of hydrogen gas then where did all these other elements come from? To answer this we must trace back to the very beginning "The Big Bang." It was astronomer Fred Hoyle who coined this term, and it remains the most likely scenario for the beginning of our universe. Regarding the big bang, theorists hypothesize that an infinitely dense, ultra tiny, speck of energy suddenly appeared. It destabilized, inflated incredibly large for a trillionth or so of a second and then blew up. The unbelievable heat energy of the explosion, literally a trillion trillion degrees hot, became all the matter in the universe as it cooled off. Remember here Einstein's famous equation. Energy equals mass times the speed of light squared. Altering this algebraic formula reveals that matter can be created from energy. During World War two we learned what happens when energy is suddenly released from matter. As the Big Bang began to cool first to come along was a hot plasma consisting of quarks, electrons and photons. The quarks eventually joined together in threes to form protons and neutrons. Protons and neutrons form the nucleus of atoms. As things cooled more the nucleus trapped an electron to orbit it. The first atom to form – hydrogen – came into existence. Hydrogen consists of one proton in the nucleus and one electron in orbit circling it.

Approximately 75% of the first atoms in the universe were hydrogen. The remaining 25% were the next simplest atom – helium. Interestingly suns create energy by fusing hydrogen atoms into helium atoms.

The next part of the story is solely the result of an attractive force called gravity. We all know what gravity is. It keeps things firmly planted on the ground rather than letting them fly off into space.

Two astrophysicists working for Bell Labs in Holmdel N.J, while working on a satellite antenna, happened to notice static coming from all areas of the sky. Arno Penzias and Robert Wilson would win a Nobel Prize for their discovery of the background radiation from the big bang. More recently space satellites have been designed to evaluate this background radiation. What was found is that the radiation is almost exactly the same throughout the universe. Thankfully for us there was a very tiny bit of clumping noted in the radiation. This clumping allowed gravity to become greater in certain areas. As gravity is an attractive force it allowed clouds of hydrogen gas to coalesce. The denser these clouds became the hotter they became. Eventually they became so dense that nuclear fusion began. The first suns were born. The universe was lit up. Now these first suns tended to be huge and burned energy rapidly. In the furnace that was their center the temperatures were so hot that atoms combined. One and one became two, two and two became four etc. The higher elements such as oxygen and nitrogen were being formed. Carbon was a very special story and will be discussed later. Eventually when all the nuclear fuel was spent the huge stars blew up. The name given to these explosions is a supernova. Supernovas littered the universe with the new elements they had formed. Gravity continued to do it's job and a second generation of stars formed from the debris of the supernova's. In their furnace they continued the process of developing higher elements. Our sun is a third generation star. The gas cloud it formed from contained these higher elements, and the gas left over formed the planets of the solar system. Our planet was lucky enough to form in what is called the "Goldilocks Zone." This zone is one that is close enough to the host sun to contain liquid water and an atmosphere that will protect the planet from ultraviolet rays and meteors. Further it was neither too hot nor too cold. Earth was also lucky enough to have a gas giant planet (Jupiter) that shields it from asteroids and comets. This last is quite important. The planet Mars began very similarly to the planet Earth, but was constantly bombarded by asteroids, and its atmosphere was destroyed.

I mentioned that the element Carbon would be discussed separately for a reason. The creation of the element Carbon is a miraculous one and is a way to introduce what is termed the "Anthropic argument." Basically what the anthropic argument says is that there were so many absolutely incredible things that were required for human life to form on the Earth that it could not have happened by chance.

In this discussion I will be relying heavily on information contained in the book *"The Science of God"* by physicist and theologian Gerald Schroeder. Gerald Schroeder is that rare brand of modern physicist who also happens to be a theologian. His attempts to reconcile physics and the Biblical book of creation (Genesis) are impressive.

Astrophysicists were literally pulling their hair out trying to figure out how the element Carbon came into the picture. Now without Carbon there would be no life as we know it. How the heck was it created? It was Fred Hoyle of "Big Bang" fame who rose to the occasion. What happens is this: First two helium nuclei join to form radioactive Beryllium. Beryllium is unstable and has an exceedingly short lifespan. It lasts for a billionth of a billionth of a second. During that brief timespan a third Helium nucleus must combine with the Beryllium to form carbon twelve, which consists of six protons, six neutrons and electrons. Now the odds of this happening are astronomical, and yet Carbon is the sixth most populous element in the universe. Hoyle's investigations found that what allowed for this is that the Beryllium and Helium nuclei have a similar resonance. We all know what resonance is. Simply think of two tuning forks. Hit one, and you can feel the vibrations in the other. Atoms that resonate at the same frequency are attracted to each other. It is this resonance that allowed Helium and Beryllium to combine in such a short period of time. Without the element Carbon chemistry would be limited to almost entirely hydrogen and helium, and no stars, no plants, no life would exist.

It was when I first read the amazing story of Carbon's creation that I sat back and thought about all the other incredibly amazing things that had to happen for life to form. When the Big Bang occurred, the contractive force of gravity exactly balanced the explosive force. If the two were not equal to the extent of one hundred twenty decimal points there would be no universe. If gravity were just a little stronger the universe would have contracted back to a point. If the explosive force were a little greater the universe would have flown apart. Either way no galaxies would ever have formed. Can you even imagine things being equal to one hundred twenty decimal points? Six decimal points represents one in a million, twelve one in a trillion. The odds of this happening by chance are like me hitting a fly ball and someone on the other side of our universe catching it. It turns out that there are about three dozen other parameters with probabilities in the many trillions that had to occur for our universe, and for life on Earth, to have formed as it is. For example, the negative charge of an electron had to be exactly balanced by the positive charge of a proton. If they were off by even a smidgeon we could say goodbye. Further, like forces repel, and yet every atom but hydrogen contains multiple positively charged protons in its nucleus. What is it that stops the protons from repelling each other and destroying the atom, and everything? It turns out that virtual particles (particles that last a mere billionth of a second before disappearing, and then appearing again) serve as strong glue. The name they have been given is Gluons, and they represent the strongest force in the universe that we are currently aware of. Now no one really understands what Gluons actually are but they are. Could this have been all random? These coincidences have led to an often-heated debate between those who believe it was God our creator who set these parameters and others who believe that it was just pure chance. I know where I now stand.

What is unfortunate about this heated debate is the amount of misunderstanding that fuels it. You see physicists often know little about theology, and theologians know little about science. This is where a person like Gerald Schroeder is helpful. Take the age of the earth for example. There are a good number of religions that believe the earth is about 6,000 years old. Apparently this number came about because of a too literal reading of the Bible. Some theologians have counted the generations of people found in the Old Testament and then extrapolated to the number of additional generations of people to arrive at this number. Schroeder, due to his training, was able to look at the bigger picture. He noted that in Genesis it mentions that Adam was created at the end of the sixth day of creation. Now if you count time from the birth of Adam 6,000 years is a fair approximation. Schroeder, however, noted that prior to Adam there were six days of creation. Once Adam was born days are twenty-four hour earth bound days. The earth is 24,000 miles in circumference and rotates around the sun at 1,000 miles an hour. The six days prior to Adam were "cosmic" days. A hint of the difference in time scales Schroeder observed in Psalm 90. "A thousand years in your sight are as a day that passes, as a watch in the night." Cosmic time and earth time are extremely different things. Einstein's theory of relativity is now the law of relativity. It has been proven so many times. The law tells us that time changes with increasing velocity and also with increasing gravity. Fortunately we do have a cosmic clock. The cosmic clock is the radiation of the Big Bang. Every time the universe doubles in size the wavelengths of light are stretched double. Scientists estimate that the universe has expanded a million million fold since the beginning. Each tick of the cosmic clock is a wavelength of light. As the cosmic clock beats a million million times slower than our earth clocks then one cosmic year represents a million million earth years. Schroeder, working with statisticians converted cosmic time into earth time and found that the six days of creation occurred in a little more then fifteen billion earth days. The first time I had learned of the estimated age of the earth was in Geology classes. Continents sit on top of huge tectonic plates. These plates move but millimeters each year. Over millions of years tectonic plates collide. When they do one rises up over the other. In this manner mountain ranges are formed. They are also the primary reasons for earthquakes. Noteworthy, sea life has been found on the tops of mountains. This suggests that mountain ranges were once under water. The face of planet Earth has changed many times since it came into existence estimated at four and one-half billion years ago.

I have already said it, but it needs being repeated, In the middle ages the Roman Catholic Church hindered scientific growth by dogmatically holding on to it's belief that the earth was the center of our solar system, and severely punishing those who believed otherwise. When this belief became untenable church teachings began to be questioned. Today we have a similar thing happening with sects of both Christianity and Judaism dogmatically holding on to beliefs that have been disproven. Continuing to teach these beliefs will only cause believers to question. This is a shame because religions have so much good to offer society and in today's mixed up world we very badly need this good.

SCIENTIFIC RESEARCH SPEEDS UP

Recent findings in quantum mechanics, cosmology and also quantum biology have made us aware of our limited understanding, and have also opened the door for a reconsideration of the paranormal.

The universe we thought we knew we now know consists of approximately seventy-percent dark energy, twenty six –percent dark matter and a mere four percent baryonic or visible matter. Ponder this for a minute. We do not understand what ninety-six percent of the universe consists of. Astrophysicist Lawrence Krauss takes us on a fascinating tour of the universe and especially dark matter and dark energy in his book *"The Fifth Essence."* Dark energy I find especially exciting. For millennia we though the universe consisted of stars, planets, moons and the empty vacuum of space. It turns out that the vacuum of empty space is not at all empty. Virtual particles, particles that come into existence for maybe a billionth of a second are constantly appearing, disappearing and appearing again. These virtual particles are thought to be responsible for the repulsive energy that is causing the universe to expand. It turns out that Einstein's "greatest mistake" was not such a mistake after all. His cosmological constant was a repulsive force that balanced off the contractive force of gravity. As the universe expands gravity weakens and the cosmological constant gains in strength and thus the universe is expanding at an increasing rate. I mentioned earlier that in a billion years the only galaxy our ancestors will see is the Milky Way. All other galaxies will be beyond our horizon. Actually this is not completely correct as the Andromeda galaxy is moving towards the Milky Way and will combine with it to form a super galaxy in a billion years or so. If anyone happens to be around it will represent an exciting time. Solar systems could collide, and planets get thrown out of their orbits and into deep space.

Now that I have given an introduction to quantum mechanics and cosmology things are going to get far stranger. Before proceeding allow me to summarize findings. Einstein showed us that energy is converted into matter and matter can return to energy. We also learned from Einstein that time is relative. Travel at the speed of light and all time stops. Speed and also gravity can influence time greatly.

When the atom was broken Pandora's box was opened. Ninety-nine point nine plus percent of every atom in your body is empty space. We are almost all entirely empty space. The fact that electrons can be shared with other atoms, forming covalent chemical bonds helps hold our bodies together and appear solid. Continuing on, particles appear to obey none of the laws of classical physics. Particles can be either a point particle or a wave. They remain in a superposition state until observed. This means that every particle exists as a statistical probability until it is observed. For example, one study shot individual photons into a light maze. There were six possible paths for the photon to travel correctly through the maze. When people observed the photons they always took only one path. When the photons were covertly observed it was found that they took all six paths simultaneously. How the heck were they aware that we were watching? Superposition, or being in multiple places simultaneously, is the finding that underlies the concept of quantum computers. It also forces us to consider the importance of our observation in determining reality. This is not a new idea. Plato's Allegory of the Cave had made the point very clearly. Plato's allegory goes like this: A group of people have lived chained to the wall of a cave for their entire lives. They are facing a blank wall. The people watch shadows projected on the wall by things passing in front of a fire behind them, and begin to designate names to these shadows. Plato's point, reality is in the eyes of the beholder.

With advances in technology we are opening Pandora's box ever further. Noted physicist John Wheeler's study I still find quite shocking. If you just consider this one study everything you thought you knew about reality is out the window. Basically what Wheeler did was this: He arranged an apparatus so that two particles were shot at a double-slit. One particle was slightly delayed. The double slit apparatus contained a venetian blind over one slit. The first particle passed the slits with the one venetian blind closed. As there was only one slit to go through we would expect to find the particle acting as a point particle when it hit the photographic plate. Here is the miracle of advanced technology. Prior to the first particle encountering the photographic plate the second particle was about to enter the slit. Just before the second particle passed the slits the venetian blind opened. With both slits opened we would expect an interference pattern for the second particle. Wheeler found that both particles presented with an interference pattern. What he is saying is that somehow the first particle was "aware" that the second particle would create an interference pattern, and it changed it's own reality from that of a point particle. This was the first study to show that past decisions can be altered by future decisions. I 'm still trying to wrap my head around this one. By this writing numerous other studies have been performed, and they all show that past decisions can be changed. Wheeler goes on to state: *"The past has no existence except as it is recorded in the present."* Understand that these studies were carried out with photons and electrons. All of the original studies making us question the reality we thought we knew have been carried out so far on particles. On the other hand remember everything in existence is created out of these particles. As of this year studies are finding that atoms and even molecules produce quantum behaviors.

ENTANGLEMENT, NONLOCALITY
AND HOLOGRAPHY

The goal of this chapter is to show how everything in the universe is related and also how universal information is permanently stored. The book of life does exist.

We will begin with "entanglement" as it is such an important concept in quantum mechanical research, and offers amazing possibilities for the future. To begin close your eyes and imagine that a laser beam shined through a crystal creates a pair of photons. Each photon is trapped inside a magnetic container. Now every particle in existence has an axis of orientation. Some particles spin one way and some another. We place one container in a lab in New York. The other particle is brought to a lab in Hong Kong. Next we alter the axis of orientation of the particle in New York by ninety degrees. Instantly the particle in Hong Kong alters, by itself, by ninety degrees. Newton and even Einstein held on to the belief that in order for one thing to influence another they must come into contact. Think of two billiard balls. In our experiment there was no such contact between the two photons. Einstein called this *"spooky action at a distance"* and refused to believe it could happen. He said: *"God will not play dice with the universe he created."* In 2004 physicist Nicholas Gisin and his group at the University of Geneva showed that entanglement occurs over 50 kilometers of fiber optic cable. Not only can it happen but so many studies have now been done confirming it that it is believed that if one particle of a pair was on earth and the other on the far side of the universe it would still happen. The term for this is "non-locality" or communication outside of time and space. Nonlocal communication is a concept that you will be hearing more and more about. Dean Radin Ph.D considers nonlocal communication to be the factor underlying paranormal behaviors. Lest you think that entanglement studies are merely an intellectual exercise know that entanglement offers incredible opportunities for quantum computing as well as communication technology and even the new field of quantum biology.

Physicist Michio Kaku, one of my favorites due to the clarity of his writing, discusses in his book *"Physics of the Future"* that teleportation is even possible. Before Scotty begins to beam people up teleportation, making use of entanglement, has only been accomplished with particles such as photons and electrons to date. Teleporting a human has significant hurdles to overcome, but may be possible a thousand years or so from now.

A husband sits in a room in California and stares intently at a picture. His wife, in a room in London, England, sits at an easel and attempts to draw the scene the husband is staring at. There are close similarities in her drawing. How can this occur? Entanglement apparently is not restricted to individual particles or atoms.

We know that entanglement occurs, but how does it occur?

Einstein's theory of general relativity predicts the existence of space-time shortcuts. We know these as wormholes. When Alice fell through a wormhole she appeared in Wonderland. When Lewis Carroll wrote *"Alice in Wonderland"* he was writing about wormholes leading to other dimensions. The wormhole concept is not new. A wormhole is thought to connect two locations in space-time or even two dimensions instantly. Recent research at leading universities suggests that when two particles are entangled a wormhole is formed between them. This wormhole allows for instant communication between them. There are competing theories out there.

I have always thought of wormholes by picturing an hourglass. The tunnel between the two ends of the hourglass is the wormhole. Wormholes can be ultra tiny and wormholes can be huge. Theoretically, two entangled photons can form a tiny wormhole and a black hole many times the size of our sun can create a wormhole. Before you think of traveling through a huge wormhole know that a planet pulled into a black hole or even a wormhole encounters gravity that is nearly infinite and will crunch that planet to the size of a grain of sand. Actually this is one theory of the multiverse. That grain of sand explodes and starts a new cycle of universe development. One interpretation of a similar theory, the big bounce theory, hypothesizes that all future universes do not develop independently, but contain information gleaned from older universes. Thus information is never lost. Future universes are smarter, and their parameters more fine-tuned. This is the one theory that makes the most sense to me. Universes expand for maybe a trillion years. Forces reverse, and contraction begins. When the universe has contracted to about the size of an atom a big bang occurs and the process starts anew. The new universe contains all information from the older universe. No matter which theory of the multiverse we choose they all require a beginning. A number of physicists have tried to develop theories that do not contain a beginning, but to my knowledge none have been successful so far. My own thought is that they will never be able to do so.

I do not wish to go too far afield, but according to physicist John Wheeler just as we understand information being stored digitally on a computer or a DVD everything that happens in the history of a universe is stored in the zero point field or quantum vacuum that makes up most of space-time. This quantum vacuum is not empty but rather a roiling sea of virtual particles that come into existence for maybe a billionth of a second. They then disappear only to return again. This not only occurs in outer space, but possibly within every cell of our bodies as well. Wheeler hypothesizes that information is stored in the minute vortexes that are created. When I discuss paranormal behaviors such as remote viewing it is thought that people can be trained to gain access to this universal database. Psychologist Carl Jung working together with Nobel Prize winning physicist Wolfgang Pauli believed this as far back as 1930.

Quantum physics, especially entanglement theory, does provide us an avenue for understanding certain paranormal behaviors.

More recent research into quantum physics has focused on the new discipline of holographic science. Holographic research together with research into entanglement has the potential to revolutionize everything we thought we knew about science. The potential is so great as to be almost beyond belief. It is definitely beyond my understanding.

While the information now to be presented is difficult to comprehend the point to be learned is this: Information is somehow stored in the interference of energy waves. This is thought to occur not only in the universe, but in the human body as well.

Much of the information I will be supplying comes from two books, along with various articles on the topic. The books are: *"The Human Hologram"* by Robin Kelly M.D, and *"The Holographic Universe"* by Michael Talbot Ph.D

In 1947, the year I was born, scientist Dennis Gabor conceived the process of holography. Unfortunately the equipment he had on hand to study holograms was inefficient. His work remained theoretical until the year 1960. In 1960 the laser became a source of coherent light. What is coherent light? Picture geese flying in a V shaped pattern. Better yet the "Blue Angels" are Navy pilots who fly in incredible precision. The planes make tight maneuvers together that are absolutely a remarkable sight to behold. Gabor's discovery is revolutionizing science. Creating a hologram requires that two beams of coherent laser light be produced from one source. One beam is aimed at the object to be represented in the hologram, while the other beam is diverted to a mirror. The light from the mirror, known as the reference beam, is then reunited with the light that had been scattered, or diffracted by the object. This results in a complex interference pattern of light waves. This pattern of interfering light waves is then recorded on a special photographic plate. When this flat two-dimensional photographic plate holding the information is exposed again to a fresh laser beam, a ghost like three-dimensional image of the object appears. The three-dimensional image is reconstructed from the information stored on the photographic plate. The beam of laser light forming the holographic image carries the information. By now most of us have been to a laser show. Information somehow stored in the interference of two laser beams creates the holographic image. Interfering energy waves not only are created by lasers, but reportedly by energy waves throughout the universe and even inside the human body. Regarding the latter, some scientists think that these interfering waves create holographic images and may be involved in consciousness.

There is a second property of the hologram that is even more important for recent research, especially research into the functioning of the human body. If you cut off a tiny piece of the photographic plate containing the image and shine a laser light on it the entire holographic image appears. A small piece contains the entire image. Just why this happens is still the subject of debate. While we may not know why it happens the fact is that it does. A tiny piece contains the total information necessary for creation of the whole image. In humans and animals DNA accomplishes this. The implications are many. Most important for our discussion is the huge information storage potential that holograms have. We all know the fact that DVD's and CD's contain stored digital information, and when a laser light is shined on the tracks we see movies and hear songs. Computer hard drives likewise store tremendous amounts of information in a digital format. Holograms have much greater storage potential.

By 2015, research has not only disputed Newtonian classical physics, but has made us question our very understanding of reality. Particles such as electrons and photons exist as waves until they are observed. When they are observed they become point particles. It is our observation that determines what we see. Entangled particles can somehow communicate with each other even if they are on opposite sides of the galaxy, and they do so instantaneously. Further photons can go into the past to alter behavior. Time itself is a relative concept and can be altered by velocity and also by gravity. Universal information seems to be permanently stored. With this in mind can we be so sure paranormal behaviors are rubbish? For that matter can we be sure of anything? When my children were young, one Christmas, they gave me a cup. On the cup is a picture of a young boy asking a question. " Does God really see everything?" The Bible tells us that God created the universe by his Word. If the Word of God represents the conscious energy of God then entanglement theory and superposition tells us that God is aware of everything, and can be everywhere simultaneously. Science is answering religious questions that we have been asking for thousands of years.

BIOLOGY CHIMES IN

The field of biology also makes us question long-held beliefs. We take so much for granted. Have you ever thought how a sperm and egg cell can, after nine months gestation, form a complete human child. These egg cells don't contain eyes and ears, and yet eyes and ears and a multitude of incredibly complex organs develop from them. The same can be said for trees and plants. When the lens of a Newt's eye is surgically removed a new lens forms from the skin on the edge of the iris. There are animals that can regenerate whole body parts. We even have a slight ability to do this. In deep sea trenches where there is no sunlight, and water pressure is incredibly strong fish and various life forms thrive. Dr. Robin Kelly discusses in his book *"The Human Hologram"* the astonishing behavior of the water bear. The water bear is an eight-legged microscopic creature that has been thriving on our planet, in extreme environments, for half a billion years. In September 2007, it was studied in the vacuum of outer space during a European Space Agency mission. The water bears not only survived but also continued to reproduce in the extremely cold and dehydrated vacuum of space. For so long we thought such a thing was impossible. We are talking about very close to absolute zero temperatures. It appears that the biological world is forcing us to rethink many cherished theories.

One study that I personally found most interesting involved termites. Once we were fortunate enough to be visited by these little creatures. They were inside a windowsill. What appeared to be millions of them occupied the entire window. They have a voracious appetite for wood. I was horrified watching them. $1200 dollars later we were rid of them. After reading the works of African Eugene Marais I came to see them in a new light. Termites in Africa and Australia build huge mounds. What is so special is the complexity of the engineering involved. The mounds are built to maintain a stable, and temperate internal temperature and are like lungs in that they allow the mound to breathe. Mainstream scientists have long held the belief that the queen termite communicates by chemical scents to the worker termites. Marais designed an experiment to test this hypothesis. He divided the termite mound with a steel plate. The queen was on one side of the mound. He then damaged both sides of the mound equally. Worker termites repaired both sides equally. This suggested to Marais that the queen was able to communicate through the steel plate telepathically. Today many call this a "hive mind." Next Marais killed the queen. Once this happened the termites wandered around aimlessly. Marais speculated that there is an organizing field, which is intimately linked to the queen. Hive minds are also found in bees, ants, wasps and vertebrates such as moles. The type of communication must be considered nonlocal as it is instantaneous and Marais study suggests not due to any direct contact such as sound waves or chemical scents. Very interesting is the fact that I did an Internet search looking for follow up studies of Marais hypothesis. I couldn't find any. Once again we see that long held theories are difficult to change. Remember it took a long while to convince people that the earth was not the center of the solar system and that vitamin C could prevent scurvy.

On the topic of the difficulty of changing long held beliefs there probably is no more important topic to discuss than evolution. I remember being in a high school biology class and listening to the teacher discuss how the precursors to organic molecules were found in warm tidal pools and it is thought that a lightening storm somehow caused them to combine into the first amino acids. From there, slowly over billions of years of mutation mammals developed followed by humans. This theory was supported by a study in 1953 by Stanley Miller. At the time Miller was a graduate student at the University of Chicago. Schroeder discusses his brilliant experiment in his book *"The Science of God."* Miller evacuated a glass tube and then filled it with the gases thought to have been present in Earth's atmosphere 3.8 billion years ago. Using electrodes placed through the walls of the flask, Miller discharged electric sparks, simulating lightening, into the gases. After a few days, a reddish slime appeared on the inner walls of the apparatus. Upon analysis, the slime was found to contain amino acids. Evolutionists jumped on Miller's study. Amino acids are the building blocks of proteins and proteins are the building blocks of life. If amino acids can be created in a flask imagine what billions of years of mutation can accomplish. Schroeder mentions that the worldwide news media reported *"life began by chance."* Twenty-five years later Scientific American magazine printed a retraction of Miller's article. Harold Morowitz, in his book *"Energy Flow and Biology"* computed that merely to create a bacterium would require more time than the Universe might ever see if chance combinations of its molecules were the only driving force. Noted astronomer Sir Fred Hoyle (remember him from the Carbon episode) had said that *"the emergence of a single-celled organism by such a random occurrence is about as likely as the assemblage of a 747 by a tornado whirling through a junkyard."* Schroeder, working with statisticians offers compelling arguments to refute claims of chance evolution of humans. He also makes note of the fact that bacteria and algae fossils were found that dated to 3.5 billion years ago. This was shortly after the introduction of water on planet Earth. All life on Earth is water based, and life developed shortly after the introduction of water. There were no billions of years for amino acids to randomly combine into life. Michael Behe, a noted professor of biology, in his book "The *Edge of Evolution"* gives a detailed, very technical evaluation of evolution and comes to the conclusion that random evolution could not possibly account for the extremely complex molecular machinery found in nature. He and many others argue that the laws of nature must contain some self-organizing force to guide evolution. The more we learn about energy fields existing throughout the universe the more likely nature has some surprises of its own.

Biologist Rupert Sheldrake has been saying this for years. He has a theory to explain how the development of all things both living and non-living comes about. Sheldrake believes that there exists in the universe informational fields that guide the development of everything. According to Sheldrake, once something is first created, such as a new crystal, an informational field is established and the field guides the. development of all future members of the class created. Sheldrake's theories seem to have been based on what has been loosely called the "100th" monkey effect. Scientists from Japan in 1952 were examining the behavior of Macaque monkeys on atolls. Apparently one monkey took sweet potatoes dropped by plane, walked to the ocean, and cleaned off the sand before eating them. Sand doesn't taste very good. Eventually other monkeys observed this and began doing the same thing. Once a certain number of monkeys had learned the new behavior monkeys on other atolls all began cleaning off the sand as well. In his book "*Morphic Resonance*" Sheldrake provides us with numerous studies that he believes suggest informational fields once developed organize future development. Sheldrake believes that his theory also explains learning. As a psychologist one such study Sheldrake makes note of had special relevance for me. I remember performing studies on rats in school. Rats learning to run a water maze in New York initially took fifty trials to find the correct pathway out of the maze. Future groups tested did better. The same study done in England found that the first group of rats tested only took twenty-five trials. This, and other studies, led Sheldrake to a theory of species-specific learning transfer. The really nice thing about Sheldrake's theories is that they are readily testable and they are being tested. British television programming has taught people in one town a skill. They then run the study in a second town to see if people there can learn it even faster. To date findings are mixed.

More recently a new field of study has begun in the field of biology. The new field studies the importance of quantum effects such as entanglement, superposition and quantum tunneling on living things. To understand quantum tunneling picture this example. You are standing with your back flat against a wall. If you stand there long enough, maybe a billion years or so, your body will fall right through the wall. The atoms in your body will line up just so with the atoms of the wall that you will slide right through the wall. Quantum tunneling does occur during our lifetime, but only at the level of particles such as photons, electrons and neutrinos. In quantum biology, the one thing studied the most so far is the process of photosynthesis. Photosynthesis is by far the most important biochemical reaction on Earth. Plants turn sunlight, carbon dioxide, and water into organic matter. Up until now the process of coherence has been achieved by lowering the temperature to near zero. At super cooled temperatures particles that usually are bouncing into each other (in electronics this is called resistance and causes lost energy) line up in a coherent dance. Nature provides us with a surprise. The process of photosynthesis involves photons from sunlight coherently traveling to reaction centers, but this is accomplished at ambient temperatures. Nature billions of years ago found a way to accomplish a feat without all of our expensive technology. If we can copy nature we could design much more efficient solar cells and solve our energy problems. We could also finally develop the elusive quantum computer.

Quantum processes are also believed to be involved in the ability of birds to navigate the Earth's magnetic field, and play an important role within the human body. Within the body we know that quantum effects are involved in enzyme-catalyzed reactions, and possibly also in our sense of smell. We are right now just beginning a much more in-depth exploration of quantum effects within the human body, and I am sure we will find that quantum mechanical effects such as entanglement, superposition and non-locality are involved throughout the body. British royal mathematician and colleague of Stephen Hawking, Roger Penrose working with anesthesiologist Stuart Hameroff holds the belief that quantum mechanical effects occurring in microtubules in every cell of the body are involved in human consciousness. Theirs and similar theories therefore consider consciousness to be due to both local and non-local effects. This would explain so much, and is the perfect lead into the next section that explores what have too long been considered paranormal effects.

PARANORMAL BEHAVIORS

I love going to the library. The headquarters branch of the Monmouth County NJ Library is huge. As I walk among the stacks of books I feel like a kid in a candy store. Reading has always been a joy for me. As a child reading was an escape from the suffering that asthma caused me. One day I picked up a book by an army officer. The book was about his experience as a participant in the military remote viewing program. This book turned out to be my introduction into the world of what we have thought of for years as the paranormal. Follow me now as I take you on a tour that I guarantee will change the way you think. I know it changed me. We will begin with remote viewing.

The book that introduced me to remote viewing was *"Reading the Enemy's Mind"* by Paul Smith. Paul was an army intelligence officer who was trained along with fellow army personnel, and some consultants, to use their minds to see what was going on inside locations both near and far. Distance, it turns out, did not matter at all.

This is such an amazing concept that I need to provide some background. According to Smith, in 1972 physicist Hal Puthoff invited artist, and psychic, Ingo Swann to Stanford University. Stanford Research International or SRI was an institute designed to pursue cutting edge research. Following some exciting initial studies Puthoff took Swann to the Varian physics building. There they were met by members of the physics faculty as well as by most physics graduate students. Puthoff had designed a fail proof experiment of psychic abilities. The building contained, several feet under the ground and heavily shielded, the Stanford Linear Accelerator. This is a particle accelerator that attempted to identify quarks or the elementary particles that in threes combine to make protons and neutrons. A slow, rhythmically moving needle traced the functioning of the particle accelerator. Puthoff asked Swann to try to make the needle move faster by the power of his mind. Swann concentrated, and the needle suddenly sped up. The physicists and graduate students thought something must have gone wrong with the apparatus. After all nobody could do that by the power of mind. Swann was next asked to make the needle slow down. He focused for several seconds and then the needle started to slow down and eventually stopped. When asked how he was able to accomplish this feat Swann replied *"I was perusing the accelerator in my mind and when I came across a gold alloy plate the needle reacted."* A paper was published regarding this experiment. At this point Russell Targ, a physicist who had long been involved in psychic research as a sideline, joined the small group. A few weeks later two men in dark suits showed up and asked Puthoff if he had written the paper. The CIA was interested. It appears that the USSR had been pouring millions of dollars into what they termed psychoenergetic research. The CIA had been concerned. It sent its own investigators to test Ingo and was thoroughly impressed by his ability to identify objects in closed boxes.

The CIA proved to be the major source of funding for the remote viewing program that was to develop. Puthoff wondered if Swann's ability to see things inside closed boxes could be expanded to much more distant psychic viewing. An experiment was designed. Swann would be randomly handed an envelope. The envelope contained the name of a city. Ingo was to tell the weather at that moment in the city. An investigator was on the phone in another room with the city's weather bureau. Ten envelopes were randomly given to Ingo. He aced all ten. Allow me to go into detail about one of the cities. Ingo was told the city was Tucson, Arizona. Paul Smith in his book reports that

Ingo, who was in a deeply relaxed state with his eyes closed, suddenly states *"A picture flashed through my mind. I am over a wet highway. Buildings are nearby and in the distance. The wind is blowing. It's cold. And it is raining hard."* Ingo had the impression that Tucson, which only gets a few inches of rain a year, was in the middle of a torrential downpour. Of course he was completely accurate, as he was in every city given to him.

This was the first realization that distance does not matter when remote viewing is occurring. A program was then developed to help participants learn to focus their minds so intensely that they could become aware of impressions. The initial training program was spread out over two years time, and concentrated on strengthening abilities associated with the right side of the brain. When the training was complete one of the participants Pat Price took one week to give a very accurate description of a secret military installation located in the Soviet Union. It was not known how accurate his description was until the Berlin Wall came down and our investigators gained first hand knowledge. From the results of the program, which went on for more than twenty years, Swann and Puthoff developed a theory to explain the findings. They had come to believe that just as a radio must be tuned exactly to a certain frequency in order to hear music, the mind of remote viewers must be tuned to a certain frequency to be able to perceive information from a "signal line." While this signal line may seem fanciful to you I assure you that many others do not find it so. Buddhists, Hindus and other groups have been speaking for millennia about what is termed the "Akashic Record." The record is thought to include all information that ever has occurred on Earth and for that matter within the universe. By entering an alternative mindset through deep meditation or drugs one can be trained to obtain information from the Akashic Record. Buddhist monks train daily from childhood to be able to achieve a state of becoming ego-less in order to accomplish this. It is only recently that I finally came to understand the concept myself. For those wishing to explore this matter further I recommend the book *"The Akashic Record"* by Synthia Andrews and Colin Andrews. For more on the integration of the new physics and Eastern Philosophy I recommend *"The Dancing WuLi Masters"* by Gary Zukov and the *Tao of Physics* by Fritjof Capra.

It is a fact that we are so consumed by the daily events occurring in our lives that we are distracting ourselves from perceiving other things. Remote viewing requires a complete clearing of the mind. Understand as well that just as many people can play baseball only a select few have the ability to make the major leagues. If you are interested in your own ability there are many, many training programs existing today. Check them out on the internet. The most important thing to me regarding Swann and Puthoff's theory is that remote viewing is not seen as psychic ability, but rather normal ability that has atrophied through years of disuse in Western Society.

As an aside, I have long considered the Bible a book of knowledge. It is a matter of not taking a too literal an interpretation but seeing the bigger picture of the writer. My personal belief is that when God directs Adam to not eat from the tree of the "Knowledge of good and evil" he is doing this to protect Adam. When Adam disobeys and develops this knowledge he is developing an ego that separates him from God. It is the ego that makes us appear as separate individuals. If there is anything that science has taught us today it is that this feeling of separateness is an illusion. All truly is one as the Buddhists have been saying for so long. The writer of Genesis knew it as well.

Getting back to the theory that abilities, such as remote viewing, have atrophied due to lack of use there is scientific evidence for this. In physiological psychology class we learned that brain cells are neuroplastic and also competitive. What this means is that when we learn new things new connections form among neurons. Second, when you stop performing a learned behavior the connections atrophy and the neurons become attached to another behavior. Psychic leg pain is a good example of this. Amputees often complain of pain in the missing leg. Investigators noticed that this often happens when the face is tickled or somehow effected. Looking on a brain map it was found that the area excited by sensations from the leg is adjacent to the area excited by sensations from the face. When the neurons receiving input from the leg no longer do so the adjacent face neurons replace the functioning of those neurons. Another example demonstrates the point that Ingo Swann made. When the brains of accountants and musicians are looked at on brain scans what they find is that there is a density of neurons on the left side of the brain for the accountants, and a density of neurons on the right side for the musicians. Practice will develop brain cells. Training in remote viewing focuses on strengthening right brain or perceptual skills. Today we are seeing a number of training programs on the internet. These programs are designed to help older people strengthen various cognitive and perceptual abilities. I am considering these myself.

Remote viewing was the beginning for me. I was hooked and wanted to learn more about behaviors that for a long time have been considered paranormal and utter hogwash.

Browsing the library I came across the book *"Edgar Cayce: An American Prophet."* Now I had never heard of Edgar Cayce and became enthralled by the first few pages of this book. Edgar Cayce was born in Kentucky to tobacco farming parents in 1877. He was poor most of his life. Early in his childhood his parents found him talking to his late grandfather. The grandfather was reported to have had psychic abilities. Edgar also reportedly spoke to imaginary friends, and his parents were quite concerned about him. I remember talking to my teddy bear as a child, but if I walked around talking to my deceased grandparents I can only imagine my parents response. Edgar dropped out of school early on. This was probably due to the fact that the other children made fun of him. Why did they do this? Because he could look at a deck of cards face down and tell you what each card was. In this regard he was a forerunner to Ingo Swann. In Edgar's days people were frightened of others exhibiting behaviors that could not be explained. If the behavior could not be explained it was considered demonic. It was only later that Sigmund Freud began the change by attributing strange behaviors to intrapsychic conflicts and unconscious processes. Carl Jung took this further by studying cultures throughout the world, and finding so many similarities among cultures that had had little if any contact that he decided there must be a "collective unconscious" that we can all tap into.

In baseball terms Edgar Cayce was a Most Valuable Player at tapping into this universal database.

What probably saved Edgar from ridicule was the fact that he became a Sunday school teacher at an early age and church was important to him throughout his life. In his later years he remarked, *"Studying the Bible and spirituality helps one with one's psychic abilities."*

What absolutely floored me about Edgar Cayce is that most of his psychic abilities were used to treat illnesses, and these psychic readings were done while he was in a trance. While he was in trance someone had to be with him to record his diagnosis and treatment recommendations. He himself remembered nothing of his trance comments. For over forty years Edgar Cayce gave readings to literally thousands of people. While he was in trance many medical doctors and luminaries of the day were at his side to record information. The accuracy of his readings was astonishing. Edgar could literally tell the body temperature of a person in another state.

Once Edgar was asked to diagnose and recommend treatment for a member of the Italian royal family. At home he went into a trance and was able to correctly diagnose the persons medical state at the time. He then went on to recommend treatment. Now comes the shock. It wasn't enough that he was able to diagnose a person in a foreign country, but he gave his diagnosis in Italian. Edgar Cayce did not speak a word of Italian, and yet diagnosed the person in a language he had no awareness of. The medical doctors present had to run out and find the local barber who was brought back to interpret. Among Edgar Cayce's general recommendations were: Maintain a balanced diet; get regular exercise; monitor your emotions and attitudes, and value the importance of relaxation and recreation. He has been called by the Journal of the American Medical Association "The father of holistic health." In his later years he was sought out by entrepreneurs who wanted advice on the stock market or who wanted him to help them locate oil deposits etc. On these things his psychic abilities were not nearly as accurate. He attributed this to his abuse of his God given abilities. It appears that he agreed to engage in these predictions not only for personal gain, but to fund his life's dream. That dream is alive today in a hospital in Virginia that is dedicated to the Cayce holistic approach to health. I recommend this book to everyone interested in not only learning about this remarkable individual, but in opening his or her mind to what Carl Jung called the "collective unconscious" or a universal database. It fascinates me that after all the years of skepticism science today is finally becoming accepting of this.

Lest anyone think that Edgar Cayce is the one and only man with psychic abilities know that throughout history, in multiple cultures, people have been mentioned as having psychic abilities. The stories of many of these people cannot be easily ignored.

Reading the book *"Uri Geller: magician or mystic"* offered an interesting insight into one person's use of his psychic abilities. Uri Geller was born in Tel Aviv, Israel. As a young child he demonstrated unusual abilities. The book reports that at age three he watched as a soupspoon bent in his hand. When he entered school he amazed the children by making watches change time.

Uri did not come from wealth, and as he grew he used his abilities to enrich himself. Uri developed a stage act that included not only psychic abilities such as bending spoons, but he had also become a master of illusions. Whenever people with supposed abilities dabble in money making enterprises whether it be showmanship or searching for oil wells like Edgar Cayce skeptics abound. Uri Geller has had more than a few skeptics throughout his professional life. He also has those who have come to believe in him. Dr. Werner Von Braun, the renowned rocket scientist and father of the United States space program had a meeting with Uri Geller, and reports that Uri "bent my ring in the palm of my hand without even touching it, and there is no scientific explanation for it."

It was suggested to Uri, that to debunk skeptics, he should undergo scientific testing. The very first scientist to evaluate Uri was in Israel. This was a specialist in electromagnetism. He was reportedly shocked when a compass placed near Uri had its needle move 90 degrees. His conclusion was that Uri Geller's electromagnetism was ten times greater than the average person. Uri underwent additional tests which showed that he could correctly read three digits in another persons mind (telepathy) and when blindfolded he correctly stated that a red car would be coming around a turn in a few seconds. Uri was also tested at the Max Planck Institute in Germany. The physicist who tested him stated that Uri demonstrated abilities that could not be explained in terms of physics. Uri then was scientifically tested in the United States. Dr. Wilbur Franklin of the physics department of Kent State University in Ohio announced after testing Uri "the evidence based on metallurgical analysis of fractured surfaces produced by Geller (a bent ring) indicates a paranormal influence must have been operative in the formation of the fractures." Off he went to Stanford Research Institute where our friends from remote viewing fame, Hal Puthoff and Russell Targ, tested Uri. They concluded that Uri Geller does have abilities that can't be explained by science.

I have spent time going over the extensive research performed on Uri Geller's abilities for one simple reason. We live in a world where materialistic and reductionist science is deeply ingrained, and multiple skeptics attack anything that seems to bring this into question. Uri Geller, unlike many other psychics, allowed himself to be tested by scientists throughout the world.

Before leaving Uri, I must introduce the event that caused him to rise to fame. Uri Geller was in the midst of a performance when he suddenly grew ill. His pulse was reportedly 170. Uri told that an enormous historic event was about to happen. He believed that Nasser, the Prime Minister of Egypt, was about to die. Twenty minutes after his prediction Cairo Radio reported that Nasser had just died of an unexpected heart attack. There had been no prior knowledge that he was sick.

I began by mentioning that Uri Geller, once he became a showman, was attacked by skeptics. Skeptics for the same reason attack Sylvia Browne. Sylvia, like Edgar Cayce, was not only a psychic who would see a person and tell them about their life, but she would go into a trance like state, and would channel a spiritual guide called Francine. Francine would give advice on a number of topics. When asked how she had all this knowledge she reportedly told interviewers that she had access to the universal records. Carl Jung had talked about a "universal source" available to all. The remote viewers trained by the military said their information came from a "source" outside of space and time. Psychics often talk of getting information from a "source". What could this source be? The Akashic records have been spoken of by various cultures and appear in books such as the Bible. The history of all that has occurred in the universe has been discussed for thousands of years. Today top physicists are beginning to talk scientifically about the universal record. Just as a DNA molecule contains information that would take millions of DVD's to store it is thought that the holographic energy background of the universe stores this universal information and is the likely "source."

Getting back to Francine for a minute. In Sylvia's book "*Contacting Your Spirit Guide*" it is mentioned that while Sylvia was in a trance and channeling Francine a group of individuals reportedly asked Francine questions. The question that interested me was "what is the purpose of this life." Francine mentioned "soul development." She went on to state that development of the soul occurs much easier in a life full of conflict than in the afterlife where there is no conflict. She further stated that this is the reason that some people choose to reincarnate. Ian Stevenson from the University of Virginia as well as Henry Grayson Ph.D have spent years interviewing individuals from around the world who have reportedly been reincarnated. Some of the stories are remarkable. One such example is that of a young child remembering details of his "other" family and also details of where he lived. With what we are learning today can anything so easily be ruled out?

If you are not yet convinced that there are people who have unique abilities consider what we have learned from Stan Lee's television program. Stan Lee is best known as the man behind Marvel Comics. Everyone today is familiar with characters such as Iron Man and The Hulk. Stan Lee has another project. He sends teams around the world to evaluate individuals who are said to have super human abilities. I have watched three episodes on television. In the first a blind young man rode a bicycle around obstacles using sonar ability similar to that used by Bats and Dolphins. The second episode showed a man sticking metal objects to his body. His body had a high level of magnetism like that of Uri Geller. The third episode that I watched showed a man lifting ten times his body's weight. I can't even lift my body weight. Just because 99.99 percent of people can't do something doesn't mean it is impossible. The same can be said of paranormal abilities.

PARANORMAL RESEARCH BECOMES RESPECTED

For years so called paranormal abilities were scoffed at. Once we had broken the atom and began to see that everything in existence is made from energy, and particles of energy such as protons, neutrons and electrons seem to obey none of the laws of physics that we had been so sure existed our thinking changed. The change in thinking meant that we might have been wrong all along regarding paranormal behaviors. Scientific researchers had for many years avoided becoming involved in paranormal research. Involvement in such research was seen as a death knell to a promising career. Academic institutions shied away from hiring such researchers, and there was very little money available to fund paranormal research.

Fortunately the times are changing and there is one man who has led that change. His name is Dean Radin Ph.D. Dean is quite an unusual man. Trained as a classical violinist he went on to receive his BS and MS degrees in electrical engineering, and then his Ph.D in psychology. For a decade or more he worked on advanced telecommunications for companies like AT&T but always kept up to date on psychic research. Eventually Dean took a risky plunge. Dean was aware that psychic research would not get him an academic position or research grants, but he kept at it. Persistence pays off.

Today he is chief scientist at the Institute of Noetic Sciences (IONS), has written four well-received books, spoken at meetings around the world, and is an adjunct professor of psychology.

In his book *"the Conscious Universe"* Dean explores in detail the research into paranormal behaviors. Paranormal simply means not understood by the laws of science we understand at this time. Dean was always inquisitive and wanted to know if there was anything to reports of psychic behaviors. Having had no psychic experiences himself, he held no bias in his scientific explorations and carefully designed and carried out statistical evaluations of studies reported. In his early work what he would do is to perform meta-analyses on already performed studies of behaviors such as ESP. For example, studies of ESP were performed on college students in several different countries. Meta-analysis would combine the scores from all subjects into one larger study. In doing so you are balancing factors such as culture and minor deviation in experimental design. What Dean found was that no matter if you were evaluating ESP card studies, dice studies, telepathy studies, remote viewing studies, or distant healing studies the results favoring "psi" ability in the general population were significantly beyond chance. Please understand that we are talking about some psychic ability not Edgar Cayce psychic ability. His books do, however, report some very exciting cases of psychic ability. I previously mentioned the study of a man sitting in a room in one country focusing on a randomly chosen picture, and his wife in another country drawing a close replica of the picture.

Dean's conclusion is that "most of the people claiming psychic abilities are either mentally ill or charlatans; however there are people who do have true psychic abilities." Additionally, his research shows a low level of psychic ability can be found in the average person, and with training this can be improved somewhat. In my mind Dean Radin, by applying a rigorous scientific method, singlehandedly has brought respectability to a field that skeptics have long attacked and dismissed.

There are currently so many studies that can be discussed. I will conclude this section by describing the studies that I find the most surprising of all. The distant healing and other studies carried out on animals and plants surprised me greatly and point up the fact that "we really are all one." In a study by Grad one-inch incisions are made into the backs of mice. One group of mice received prayer from a healer. The other group of mice received no prayer. The mice prayed for healed much faster. Grad and his group were visionaries. In one study he had normal and depressed individuals hold a flask of water that was used to feed seeds. They held the water for several minutes and focused on the seeds growing. The seeds watered by the normal individuals grew well. The psychotically depressed individuals seeds grew very poorly. This and a host of other studies Grad performed seems to back up the "green thumb" effect. I have always believed in this one. His studies also offered support for the field of distant healing.

While these studies were shocking Tompkins and Bird described the most shocking of all in the book "*The Secret Life of Plants*". The authors discuss the work of Cleve Backster. Cleve Backster was an expert with lie detectors. Backster discovered that plants react emotionally in ways similar to humans. For example, he hooked up a lie detector to a plant. When he had the thought "I will burn the plant with a match" the lie detector needle reacted. The plant seemed to be aware. When he did light the match and approach the plant the needle jumped again. " When he thought that he would not burn the plant the lie detector calmed down". Backster did one study where he ground up the leaves of a plant and still the ground up leaves responded to human emotions. He then went on to perform a series of experiments in which he tested leukocytes (white blood cells) taken from his test subjects. The procedure for obtaining the cells had been perfected earlier. Backster moved the culture collected in a test tube to a distant location. He then placed the electrodes of the lie detector on the culture. Next he provoked emotional responses in his test subjects. When his subjects reacted physiologically the test cultures did also. The lie detector needle swung when the test subjects were looking at an emotionally arousing picture. One of the pictures was a nude shot of Bo Derek, and the test subject a young man. I would have made that needle jump as well. Backster and his colleagues reportedly toured the country performing studies with different instruments and different plants. Each time they observed similar findings. Backster and Aristide Esser, the director of medical research at the Rockland State Hospital in New York, at different times, together showed that when a subject lies in front of a plant that is hooked up to a lie detector the graph responds. The plant apparently knew when the people were lying. This last finding I find so hard to understand. For that matter in writing this book there have been many things that I am still trying to understand. I will tell you that I now have a healthy respect for plants and when I go into my vegetable garden I smile and talk pleasantly to the growing plants.

I know the science section contained a lot of extremely difficult information to try to understand, but now is the time to integrate what science has told us with the information from studies such as Clive Backster's. Science showed us that elementary particles of energy somehow or other are aware of human intentions, and can change their reality from a point particle to a wave based on information. Backster's studies have shown us that plants and even blood cells respond to our emotions. Add to this the fact that we have learned from science that every particle of energy is entangled and entangled particles somehow are able to communicate. What we have learned is that everything in the universe exhibits "awareness." Everything seems to have a form of consciousness. Every cell in the human body is aware of the goings on in every other cell. It is thought by renowned scientists such as Dr. Candace Pert that this explains the coherence found in the body and is the reason that the entire body can react so quickly to stimuli. Unfortunately there are a good number of scientists, especially neuroscientists, who believe that communication among cells is local communication and requires direct contact between neurotransmitters and hormones and cells. This is old paradigm thinking and is deeply ingrained. While this does occur the communication is not nearly fast enough to explain the speed with which there is communication within the body. Local and nonlocal communication must occur. The relatively new field of psychoneuroimmunology suggests that what affects one aspect of the body (mental or physical) affects all aspects of the body. This has been proven in numerous studies. It is also the reason I incorporate spirituality and positive thinking in my treatment of physically disabled patients. Depressive thoughts such as hopelessness undermine healing. Depressive thoughts have even been found to impact negatively on the growth of plants. Everything truly is one.

MEDIUM RESEARCH

Back to the library I went. There was a different type of paranormal behavior that I wished to investigate next. My personal inquisitiveness led me to a book titled *"The Afterlife Experiments"* by Gary Schwartz, and Linda Russek. Gary and Linda are psychologists. Gary is the director of Arizona University's Human Energy Systems Laboratory. This book is an absolute must read for anyone interested in the question of the survival of consciousness after death. Following Dean Radin's example the researchers were careful to rule out any competing hypotheses that could have accounted for their findings. What they did was to put together a "Dream Team" of mediums. The mediums (George Anderson, Laurie Campbell, John Edwards, Suzanne Northrup and Anne Gellman) were then put through a series of very carefully designed experiments to rule out any fraud or deceit in their readings of "Sitters." The results are staggering. When five out of five mediums all say very similar, and highly descriptive, things about a person they had never met before the scientist in me was literally floored. How could this be? Even more surprising a medium correctly got highly personal information about an individual that she was going to have a phone reading with one-half hour prior to the actual reading. Again I note that the researchers went out of their way to rule out any possibility of competing hypotheses.

In one of their studies all five mediums correctly mentioned to a woman, seated in a separate room, that she had recently lost a son. One medium went even further. John Edwards mentioned to the woman that not only had she lost her son, but he heard a sound like a bang when thinking of him. From his experience this suggested to Edwards that the son committed suicide by shooting himself. The woman was in shock. Edwards had got it right. In his book *"One Last Time"* John Edwards has a fascinating theory. John believes that in our bodies energies are restricted to the speed of light. When we pass over, however, the spirit is now at a higher energy level. It takes extreme sensitivity and training for a medium to "tune in to the energy of the spirit." Spirits likewise need to work to get through to the medium. This would explain why the military's remote viewers and others mention that the information they receive comes in piecemeal and as if there is much static. It also explains why they are sometimes wrong in interpreting this piecemeal information.

I probably have already mentioned it, but I am going to do it again. Our body consists of organs. Organs, such as the heart are made up out of tissues. Tissues are made up out of cells. Cells are made up from protons, neutrons and electrons. Protons, neutrons and electrons are made out of energy. Everything in existence in the universe is created from energy, and scientists aren't even sure exactly what energy is. How can we say anything therefore is impossible?

From reading books such as James Van Pragh's *"Talking to Heaven"* it has become clear to me that true mediums are sensitive individuals who have trained their minds to ignore extraneous material and focus intensely. Unfortunately, because there are so many frauds out there, true mediums tend to get lumped in with them by the public.

It is the new paradigm of science that has made me do a complete turnabout in my own thinking. If photons can be in multiple places at the same time, and demonstrate a form of awareness, then who are we to doubt that there are people who can speak to spirits? Energy can be altered but never destroyed. While Schwartz's and Russek's research may have been the most thorough research so far on mediums it is not the first. More than a century ago the eminent William James and his colleagues investigated a woman named Mrs. Piper. Piper claimed to be able to receive information from departed individuals. William James was thoroughly impressed and came to the conclusion that Mrs. Piper was a genuine "white crow" that disproved the law that "all crows are black." Schwartz and Russek have identified many more "white crows" and there are undoubtedly many others out there. The military's remote viewers are now retired and training people all over the world. Soon I expect we will find more and more "white crows."

Research into mediums is now ongoing. One organization that I am a member of is the Institute of Noetic Science (ions.org). Besides offering a forum for members to discuss ideas it is at the forefront of research into paranormal behaviors. Dean Radin is the chief scientist and he, other scientists from IONS, along with scientists from the University of California and the Windbridge Institute recently were involved in a new study of mediums. Six Windbridge Certified Research Mediums were tasked with two separate activities. Strict scientific procedures were followed to rule out any competing hypotheses.

In the first the mediums were given the first name of a deceased individual and then were asked twenty-five questions about this person.

Their responses were transcribed and scored for accuracy by individuals who knew the deceased persons well. Three of the four mediums used in this part of the experiment yielded statistically significant results. The things they knew about the deceased individual could not have happened by chance. The second part of the experiment involved the mediums being guided to experience four distinct mental states. These were: thinking about a known living person (recollection), listening to a biography (perception), thinking about an imaginary person (fabrication), and interacting with a known deceased person (communication). The reason given for this protocol is that skeptics will often argue that the mediumship mental state is akin to making up an imaginary person or remembering previously obtained information.

The mediums were wired up, and electrocortical activity was measured during each state. Statistically significant differences among the four conditions were found in all mediums participating. The scientists state in their article (*Frontiers in Psychology, 2014*) that the mediums are involved in a subjective experience that cannot be explained as imagination or some other form of known recall. Research into this new and exciting area continues.

NEAR DEATH AND OUT OF
BODY EXPERIENCES

Near death and out of body experiences have been discussed in cultures around the world for millennia. While scientifically evaluating them has been next to impossible things may be changing in the future. Today there are multiple organizations that are collecting and codifying information on both from around the world. The Near Death Research Foundation (nderf.org) is one of many that are collecting such information. What has been found to date is that there are similarities to the reported information given by people from different cultures.

I will begin by evaluating near death experiences. Pediatrician Melvin Morse has been on the forefront of researching children who have experienced near death. In his book "*Where God Lives*" he discusses the near death experiences of the children he studies as well as the neuroscience that he believes supports his theory of there being an area of the brain that quantum mechanically interacts with the universal consciousness that he believes many call "God." Morse's book is such a positive read. Not only does he give such interesting case examples such as a young boy near death who leaves his body and visits his parents in the hospital waiting room, and later correctly tells them what they talked about while he was being operated on, but he follows such children throughout their lives. What Morse finds is that children who experienced near death have survived with a new and very healthy mentality. His children, as he calls them, avoided drugs, promiscuity and other teenage problems. As young adults most were called to healing professions.

Now skeptics seem to universally try to explain near death experiences as the anesthesia wearing off or the bright lights above the operating table. From what I have read of skeptics I have come to see them as deeply entrenched in the materialist and reductionist thinking of the last three hundred years. To this way of thinking the only things that matter are those things that can be seen or touched. Such people have therefore come to see consciousness as purely the result of chemical reactions within the brain. When the brain is dead there is no more life. I long remember a philosophy class in college where the professor mentioned to us that if a radio no longer works does that mean that the radio waves disappear. Likewise if the brain no longer functions does that mean that conscious waves disappear. I got the point. We have come to identify ourselves completely with our physical bodies. Many long held beliefs, such as the Earth being the center of the universe, have been shattered by science. I believe the new paradigm of science in quantum mechanics is shattering many more long held beliefs today.

Getting back to near death experiences, there is one case that I believe cannot be explained by all the skeptics in the world. The case of Pam Roberts is discussed in the book *"Light and Death"* by Michael Sabom. Michael Sabom is a cardiologist and currently a near death researcher. I will summarize the case here

Pam Roberts was a singer and musician. She developed a large aneurysm in an extremely risky area of her brain. Fortunately for her she was referred to the Barrows Neurological Institute in Phoenix, Arizona. There the institute director had developed a surgical procedure to treat patients like Pam. The procedure required her body temperature to be lowered to sixty degrees; her heartbeat and breathing stopped; her brainwave flattened, and the blood drained from her body. In other words she was clinically dead and only kept alive by machines. With no blood in Pam's brain it was relatively easy to remove the aneurysm and seal off the artery. The difficult part was bringing her back to life. The blood bypass machine was turned back on and warm blood was sent back into her body. Eventually her brain stem and then the higher levels of her brain began to show electrical activity. Next, the previously inactive heart monitors began to show the disorganized activity of ventricular fibrillation. Her heart was shocked several times to return normal heart rhythm. When Pam was stable enough she was disconnected from the blood bypass machine. A life had been saved. What makes this case so noteworthy are the steps taken to make sure there was no brain activity. She was completely anesthetized and the blood removed from her brain. There is no way skeptical neuroscientists could say for her to have overheard things said by the doctors and nurses while she was being operated on.

When she was able to speak Pam began mentioning things that went on during the operation. *"Why did you tell this nurse that and the other one that etc.?"* The doctor looked at her questioningly. How was it possible that she knew all these things? When asked, Pam told the doctor that the whole time she was being operated on *"I was looking over your shoulder watching you operate on my body. When I looked over your shoulder it wasn't like normal vision. I saw everything much brighter, more in focus, and so very clear."*

In his book *"Where God and Science Meet"* Patrick McNamara mentions a startling study. People who had had heart attacks and required resuscitation were divided into two groups. One group contained those who did not report an out of body experience. The other group included those who did report having an out of body experience. The groups were then interviewed regarding their recollections of the operating room. The group that did not report having an out of body experience guessed based on past knowledge of what an operating room was like. The group that reported having had an out of body experience gave much more detailed accounts of the operating room. There is one particular person who stood out. At the end of the interview the interviewer mentioned to this person that he had never mentioned the paddles that were used to shock his heart. The man went on to say *"doctor there were no paddles in the room, but they did put two disks against my chest and I saw my body jump."*

There are two more cases that I now wish to discuss. They couldn't be more different than Pam Roberts. Whereas Pam was a singer and entertainer, Eben Alexander M.D was a highly respected neurosurgeon and a skeptic, and Mary Neal M.D was a highly trained orthopedic surgeon and also an admitted skeptic.

I will start with Dr. Alexander. His book *"Proof of Heaven"* gives us an in-depth look at Eben. Eben Alexander was born into a family of neurosurgeons. His father was one of the top men in his field, and Eben adored him and wanted to follow in his footsteps. Eben loved science and trained at the best schools. He then went on to work in the best hospitals. Eben authored or coauthored more than one hundred fifty book chapters and papers for peer-reviewed medical journals and presented his findings at more than two hundred medical conferences around the world. He was the epitome of a man of science. Like most neurosurgeons Eben was trained to consider the brain the sole source of consciousness. He thought it is true that scientists have not yet figured out how this electrically charged machine that we call the brain produces consciousness, but Eben felt it was only a matter of time before they would understand it. It was clear to him. In his book he describes a typical case. *"A patient comes in with headaches and diminished consciousness. You obtain and MRI (magnetic resonance image) of her brain and discover a tumor. You place the patient under general anesthesia; remove the tumor, and a few hours later she's waking up to the world again. No more headaches. No more trouble with consciousness pretty simple."*

Eben loved the simplicity. He had been thoroughly trained to avoid sloppy thinking. If a fact could be accepted as tangible and trustworthy it was accepted. If it could not be so proven then it was rejected. This is the hallmark of materialistic thinking. This approach left no room for the soul and spirit. It left no room for the continuance of consciousness and personality after the brain that supported these characteristics of life stopped functioning. It certainly left no room for an afterlife.

Eben did attend church with his family on Easter and Christmas, but was an avowed skeptic. He was a skeptic due to his medical training, and also to his life operating on patient's brains. That was about to change.

One morning as he lay in bed next to his wife he suddenly felt a sharp pain in his back. Over time the pain worsened. His young son came into the room and just touched Eben's head. Eben screamed from the pain that ensued from just a gentle touch. He was stubborn and wanted to avoid going to the hospital but eventually his wife called for an ambulance. On the way to the hospital he suffered a prolonged grand mal seizure. The doctors were perplexed. None of the usual tests explained what they were seeing. Finally a spinal tap was performed. Instead of a clear fluid what came out was pus. Eben was in serious trouble. The long and short of it is that Eben had contracted a gram-negative bacterial meningitis. From my own postdoctoral training in pharmacology and medical science I can tell you this is the absolute worst thing to have contracted. Gram-negative bacterial meningitis is a highly aggressive disease that, in cases such as his, kills about ninety percent of patients. The ten percent that live do so as vegetables. The bacteria literally eat away at the cortex of the brain that is responsible for all higher brain functions. Over time they eat away at the deeper or primitive brain that is responsible for basic life functioning. This is not at all something that you want.

What is so surprising is that the disease affects less than one in ten million healthy adults each year. There was no clear protocol for the doctors to know how to treat it in Eben. Within a short period of time Eben's cortex was not functioning at all. The only brain functioning found on tests was primitive reflexes, and even these were diminishing.

During the week that Eben remained in a coma family members were at his side praying for him. Eben, on the other hand, was experiencing something that he never believed was possible. He was outside of his body experiencing the oneness of multiple dimensions and multiple universes. He was learning that the unconditional love of God suffuses the entirety of all that there is. He learned that some evil is necessary in this world for the spirit to grow. On the day that his treating physicians were speaking to his family about discontinuing antibiotic treatment since it didn't seem to be helping and his condition was "in the hands of God", he suddenly opened his eyes and spoke. For the first week or so, as his brain came back online, he experienced what is called an ICU psychosis. He hallucinated and rambled on incoherently much of the time. He didn't remember people's names etc. While the aftermath of my stroke seven years ago was nowhere as bad I can remember speaking to my family and I would mean to say one thing but the wrong words would come out. Slowly over a few months this disappeared in both of us. The brain has been injured and takes time to "reboot." In Eben's case his recovery was a million fold more surprising than in mine.

Eben returned as a changed man. He now knew firsthand that consciousness does exist outside of the brain. As a scientist he carefully ruled out all the competing hypotheses that neuroscientists had developed to explain out of body experiences. His was now a "mission."

He has since devoted his life to helping other professionals come to understand what he had experienced firsthand.

It is in this mission that I feel a strong bond to Eben Alexander.

While I myself have never had the experience that Eben had, the scientist in me has done nonstop research into the new physics and into the paranormal for seven straight years. I have met with professionals who have reported out of body and other paranormal experiences as well as have read everything I could get my hands on. I now strongly believe that the new paradigm of physics is consistent not only with paranormal behaviors but with the immortality of consciousness, and even life after death. As Eben Alexander, nowhere in my professional training, either pre or postdoctoral, did I ever hear the words spirituality or God mentioned. In western society this is due to the dogmatic belief in materialism and reductionism. Regarding reductionism we seem to have gotten to the very smallest particles of matter and all we did was open a Pandora's box. I will describe once again to make the point, particles that are way too small to be seen can somehow communicate, can be in multiple places at the same time, and can alter their reality based on our observation of them. Professionals can accept this but some still doubt a creator. Like Eben I also see myself as on a mission to educate people, and I also am finding it so frustrating at times to break through the materialistic brainwashing they have received.

I chose one more near death experience to present. Mary Neal M.D is an orthopedic surgeon living in Jackson Hole, Wyoming. What makes Mary Neal's case so different than Eben Alexander's or Pam Robert's is that their near death experiences happened as they suffered life threatening illnesses, and were in a hospital. Mary Neal almost died in a kayaking accident in the remote mountains of Chile, and had her experience while submerged and unable to breathe. Her life is described In the book *"To Heaven and Back"*.

Mary Neal grew up in a town in Michigan. A creek ran through her backyard. Mary describes the hours she spent swimming, ice-skating, fishing and exploring. Throughout her life she has always been athletic.

Her father was a medical doctor and her mother a housewife. The family went to church on Sunday's, but religion played a small role in her upbringing. At the age of fourteen her life was shattered when her parents divorced. Like many teenagers in situations like this she began to rebel. One night Mary and some friends were driving to a party when they got into a serious car accident. The car was totaled but Mary walked away with only some bruises. As an undergraduate pre-med major Mary got a job in a dive shop. She always loved swimming and now wanted to learn how to dive. She went with the diving school to Florida and did a dive at night together with an instructor. Not realizing it they entered an underwater cave and couldn't find their way out. The air in their tanks was almost depleted. Mary prayed to God and suddenly a little fish appeared before them. They followed the fish out of the cave. The air in their tanks ran out just as they were nearing the surface. This experience increased her belief in God's mercy and also her belief in Guardian Angel's. Medical school and scientific training however tended to make her skeptical and begin to doubt once more.

She married a man who, like her, was an avid kayaker and athletic. When their children were old enough to be left alone with the family nanny (both her and her husband were orthopedic surgeons) they went on a kayaking vacation with friends to the mountains of Chile. The day they were to leave for home her husband awoke with serious back pain and backed out of kayaking. Mary went by herself. When she arrived at the remote destination she was surprised to see that there were some inexperienced kayakers with the group. The course they would be attempting was difficult. There were ten and twenty foot drops down waterfalls, dangerous rapids, and also boulders to be avoided. The first person to attempt a drop lost control of her kayak. She ended up trapped between two boulders. A second person had difficulty as well. Mary's kayak collided and ended up underneath the trapped kayak. She was trapped in her kayak, submerged, and unable to breathe. The other kayaker's didn't realize she was missing for many minutes, and when they did they had difficulty getting to her due to the rushing water. Eventually they were able to free her from her kayak. Just as Mary felt herself being pulled by her rescuers she reported hearing a "pop". It was at this point that she felt her soul leave her body. Mary found herself confronted by a welcoming committee of fifteen to twenty human spirits sent by God. Eventually she realized that they were family and friends who had passed on. Each spirit was dazzling and radiant in appearance. Mary felt an overwhelming sense of unconditional love and joy. She found herself able to communicate with the spirits but not with spoken words. They were sent to guide her along a path. Just as she was about to enter a great hall she heard the words *"It is not your time; you have work yet to do."* The spirits then guided her back to her body and she entered it. The next thing she remembered was opening her eyes and seeing her friends all about her. Her ordeal was far from over. She was in a remote area of the Chilean mountains. There was no hospital nearby. She had suffered severe physical injuries as well as a lack of oxygen. The trip home was a nightmare but also a miracle. When Mary was brought to a hospital in Wyoming she was diagnosed with severe pneumonia as well as acute respiratory distress syndrome. This meant that not enough oxygen was getting to her body. Her multiple orthopedic injuries were not life threatening. The lack of oxygen was. The husband was told that she probably would not live the night. Friends and church members rushed to the hospital and prayed all night for her. Mary Neal survived and healed. Today she continues her practice of medicine, and feels her experience has made her a better person. Whenever possible she shares the love of God with patients, friends and groups she speaks to. Mary stresses the fact that there is purpose to this life, and that purpose has to do with loving God, loving your fellow man, and strengthening the soul.

While these cases may have been exceptional many, many more cases can be found in the literature. People who have been given days to live have suddenly and unexplainably gone into complete remission. Allan J. Hamilton M.D, a neurosurgeon and oncologist discusses a number of cases where patients had brain cancer and were not expected to live much longer, and then suddenly went into remission. His book " *The Scalpel And The Soul* " gives us hope. One of the cases he discusses actually brought me to tears. While Allan Hamilton was in training he was assigned to a burn unit. A nine-year-old boy name Thomas was brought in. Thomas had been electrocuted and horribly burnt over his entire body. Skin from cadavers was used to cover his body and protect him while he lie in a coma. Unfortunately his immune system rejected the skin. Suddenly, and quite unexpected, his 42-year old father had a heart attack and died. His wife authorized the doctors to cover Thomas' body with his fathers skin. This skin was not rejected, but Thomas went on to develop a blood infection, and was not expected to live. One night after working for many hours Dr. Hamilton fell asleep in the on-call room. Two hours later loud banging on the door awakened him. A nurse was shouting its Thomas come quickly. Dr. Hamilton expected the worse. When he arrived at Thomas' room he saw Thomas trying to throw off the bonds that held him in place. Dr. Hamilton removed the tube from his mouth. Thomas shouted: "*what is wrong with my father?*" Dr. Hamilton not wishing to upset him said nothing is wrong. Thomas replied "*then why is he just standing there and not speaking?*" Dr. Hamilton told Thomas the truth about his father. Thomas said: "*oh then it is his ghost. Now the ghost is waving to me and leaving* the room." Thomas survived and when last seen was back in school and on the honor roll. Although horribly disfigured he smiled and seemed happy. Allan Hamilton was no longer a skeptic from that day.

The Institute of Noetic Science (<u>IONS.ORG</u>) has, in recent years, collected evidence of spontaneous remissions from life threatening illnesses from medical journals covering twenty languages. As of 2014 they had collected 3500 such cases. More such cases are constantly being found.

Traditional medicine has extended our lifespans and saved so many lives but it cannot explain all healings.

In the book "*Autobiography of a Western Yogi*" by Donald Waters the story of a young American man was told. The young man in question was the son of an American doctor and was extremely inquisitive. He traveled to Northern India in search of answers. There he studied for years under the tutelage of a master teacher or Yogi. I applaud him for his perseverance but I cannot even fathom myself sleeping under the bed of my teacher for years. I know I am not alone in that. We are so used to our comforts. The book mentions many incredible things the Yogis were able to do, but one in particular fits right into this book. The master teacher becomes very sick and is taken to the local clinic. The student and a number of prominent Yogi's stay at his bedside and carry out spiritual rituals. The doctor kept asking them to leave. "*The patient was brain dead when you brought him in.*" They ignored the doctor and kept up their prayers. After forty days the Yogi opened his eyes and reportedly said: "*Why did you not let me leave? It was so pleasant, and so peaceful. I was without pain and flying around the world enjoying every minute.*" The doctor entered the room and saw the patient conversing with the assembled Yogis and was in shock. Reportedly the doctor asked permission to join them as a student and took leave of his medical practice. He felt he could help more people with their training than with traditional medicine.

The Yogi was "out of body and flying around without pain." At the same time his physical body was brain dead. In this country when you wish to learn about out of body experiences there is one primary place to go. That place is the Monroe Institute in Virginia. During their training the military remote viewers were taken there by Ingo Swann.

Bob Monroe has been at the forefront of out of body experiences for over forty years. Monroe's book *"Journeys Out Of The Body"* has become a classic in the field and provides an interesting picture of the man and his theories. Monroe himself is such an interesting person. For much of his adult life he was respected as a radiobroadcasting executive. In this regard he was responsible for the production of a large number of radio programs, became active in radio station ownership, cable television, and also in an ongoing research program. It is in this last activity that Robert Monroe became so well known. He was long interested in music and specifically the effects of sound frequencies on the human brain. While personally investigating sleep-learning he had an interesting experience. His first book *"Journeys Out Of The Body"* describes these in detail. Robert found himself leaving his physical body. Now, unlike those experiencing this as a result of a near death experience his initial experience was anything but pleasant. Instead of being met by loved ones and feeling unconditional love he was frightened and had what the psychologist in me would term nightmarish experiences. His memories of these early experiences, that he immediately made note of, actually scared me. This didn't stop him from continuing. Robert Monroe was a scientist. Monroe, little by little, would learn to control his out of body experience and what brought it on. His last book *"Ultimate Journey"* published in 1994, describes his research assisted by physicians, psychologists, engineers, educators and other professionals.

The culmination of his research led to the development of what is termed "Hemi-Sync" technology. Different frequencies of sound are played into opposing ears. This audio technology is thought to produce coherent brain waves (think back to holographic research). Monroe believed that certain combinations of frequencies enhanced learning, others enhanced sleep, and others enhanced expanded states of consciousness. Out of body experiences are one expanded state of consciousness. Research at his institute does provide evidence that coherent brain waves produced by Hemi-Sync technology increases whole brain functioning. Interestingly deep meditation has been found to accomplish this also. Paul Davies in his book on the military remote viewing program discusses his team's experiences at the Monroe Institute with Hemi-Sync technology. Some, but not all of the students did have out of body experiences while there. Presently the Monroe Institute is leading the research into what has for too long been termed paranormal behaviors. OBE's are no longer being scoffed at.

SPECULATIONS ON BRAIN FUNCTIONING

There are many who believe the brain functions on two levels, and this explains what has long been considered paranormal behaviors. Pediatrician Melvin Morse is one of these. He believes that an area of the brain communicates quantum mechanically and non-locally with the universal consciousness, and this is responsible for what is often considered experiences of God. Morse reminds us that for centuries the right side of the human brain was the dominant side. The right side was more important for survival skills. With the development of writing, more effective means of communication, and industrialization, the left or more logical side became dominant. This has happened predominantly in western societies to date. In less developed societies the right side of the brain is still dominant and so are reports of miraculous healings and visions. Consistent with this the military remote viewers were put through a two-year training program that focused on strengthening behaviors associated with the right side of the brain, and after completing the program were able to do astounding things. Ingo Swann's theory is that lack of use caused certain behaviors mistakenly considered paranormal to atrophy.

Reading Morse's theory made me remember back to physiological psychology class where we learned of neuroscientist Wilder Penfield's studies where he applied electrical shocks to different areas of the brain. When Penfield shocked the right temporal lobe he found that people reported seeing bright lights, viewed memories from their lives, and some experienced an out of body sensation. Morse calls the right temporal lobe "the God spot," and believes that it interacts quantum mechanically with the universal consciousness.

Anesthesiologist Stuart Hameroff and Britain's eminent mathematician Sir Roger Penrose have proposed a theory as to how the brain functions on two levels. They hypothesize that the brain acts locally by the action of neurotransmitters, and non-locally (quantum mechanically and in contact with the universal consciousness) through miniscule structures called microtubules that are part of every neuron.

Is their theory correct? This I do not know, but what I do know is that research into this exciting area began slowly but today more and more scientists are now participating in it. What I myself never understood is: the brain is made up of cells, and cells of atoms. Atoms are made up out of inanimate sub-atomic particles. Therefore, how could inanimate particles create consciousness. According to many of today's physicists and philosophers the answer is that sub-atomic particles contain what must be considered "Awareness" and consciousness may be the only true reality. Thus the brain itself is viewed as a receiver and moderator of consciousness. If a radio breaks the information remains available. The brain is seen similarly. According to physicist John Wheeler information is never lost throughout the universe. According to singer and songwriter Bob Dylan the world is a-changing.

REINCARNATION

I wasn't intending to write about reincarnation, until reading an interesting hypothesis presented by psychologist Dr. Henry Grayson. Most of the world believes in reincarnation and there are absolutely amazing stories where young children have remembered the name of their previous family, where they lived, and other details. Edgar Cayce too was a devout believer in reincarnation. Henry Grayson has taken an approach that is more in line with current thinking in theoretical physics. We know from Freud and developmental psychologist Jean Piaget that children prior to age five or six tend to be more open to right brain oriented thinking, and to be very much in touch with their mystical side. Grayson's hypothesis states that young children sometimes may be in touch with memories of a past individual stored in the universal database. Beyond age five or six these memories start to fade as do memories of near death experiences. This is consistent with developmental psychologist Jean Piaget's findings that age six ushers in the stage of concrete thinking. In today's day and age with computers I would lower that age. I have seen five year olds who can do things with computers that are beyond me. Grayson's is quite an interesting hypothesis. It is one that I had never considered before but, with our current thought considering a universal database, is worth consideration. What I do know is that there are so many stories of children and adults remembering past lives that there is an answer. It would be a mistake to just write these people off.

Throughout history change happens slowly. People tend to hold on to beliefs dogmatically until one day a creative thinker such as Copernicus comes along. Our creative thinker has to fight the prevailing belief system to be heard. Skeptics abound, and can make his or her life hard. Soon others come to see the truth in his or her new beliefs, and they begin to explore the issue. Eventually they prevail, and the truth is heard. The new paradigm of science is still in the very early stages of development, and will eventually change the way we have looked at the world for the last three hundred years. Our materialistic understanding of reality will be the very first thing to be replaced. Grayson's hypothesis may be accurate.

IMPLICATIONS FOR HEALTHCARE

As a clinical psychologist with training in pharmacology and medicine healthcare is a primary concern of mine. Therefore I would now like to discuss the implications of the new paradigm of science for healthcare. Personally I have never been one to immediately accept something just because it came from a respected source. This reveals the scientist in me. I want to see things as hypotheses to be tested. If the findings are strongly favorable and are replicable I will accept the hypothesis. If the findings are not favorable or replicable I cannot accept the hypothesis as stated. This I have done and now believe that the new paradigm of science has strong implications for healthcare. Follow along with me now and I am sure you will agree.

The very first place that I had realized the implications for healthcare was in the book "*Reinventing Medicine*" by Dr. Larry Dossey. Larry Dossey, in his first year of medical practice reports having had several prophetic dreams over a few days. In the first of these he vividly saw in his dream a young boy in a doctor's office. The doctor was trying to place an apparatus onto the boy's head. The young boy struggled mightily and eventually the doctor had to give up. The very next day Larry Dossey met a colleague who told him that his son had run a high fever and went into seizure. The father was sure that it was the fever that had caused the seizure, but to be safe arranged to have an EEG performed on his son. The neurologist they chose specialized in children and never before had he failed to successfully perform the test, at least not until this day. The son struggled so much with the placement of wires on his head that the testing had to be put off. The colleague told Dossey that no one knew of the seizure and EEG but himself, his wife, and the neurologist. Over the next few days Dossey reports having had two more prophetic dreams. Again the very next day he witnessed the things he had dreamt come true. As with the first dream there was no way for Larry Dossey to have known of the events that occurred. Now Larry Dossey had been trained to believe that consciousness works through the brain and is a process requiring neurotransmitters. Therefore how could a dream of future events be possible given that he had no way of knowing of the events he had dreamt of. Dossey tells us that never again did he have such prophetic dreams, but they had opened his eyes to possibilities, and he began reading everything he could about prophetic dreams and eventually the new paradigm of science. As a result of his study he came to believe that traditional medicine has placed undue constraints on itself, and it is time for medicine to enter the twenty-first century.

Dossey, in his book *"Reinventing Medicine,"* outlines for us three era's of medicine. Each era required a qualitative change in how we approach medicine. The first era Dossey tells us came about in the mid 1800's. At that time medicine began to become a science. Medicine became a method of practice supported by respected theories and under girded by the accepted laws of nature. At this time consciousness was something poorly understood and not accepted as an avenue for medical research. Around the year 1900 Freud was able to debunk the idea of demons being responsible for emotional problems. This was a tremendous leap. Reportedly many of the "witches" burned at the stake in Salem were emotionally disturbed individuals. Freud, a neurologist did however strongly believe that the brain was responsible for consciousness and consciousness worked through physical processes. Psychoanalysis was his means of investigating personality development, and cocaine appears to have been an adjunct to his treatment. This last needs to be understood in context. In Freud's day the most common drugs used to cure ailments were opiates and cocaine. Cocaine was even an ingredient in Coca Cola.

In the mid 1900's we entered era two in medicine. Era two was brought about largely by the placebo effect. As a practicing clinical psychologist I was always surprised when a patient suffering a full blown panic attack would take a minor tranquilizer and less than five minutes after taking it would suddenly calm down. Orally consumed pills must be digested and work their way through the liver and into the bloodstream. This process usually takes about fifteen to twenty minutes, and yet after five minutes the patient often feels fine. From my own life I experienced this placebo effect myself at an early age. Shortly after my grandmother, who lived with us, died I became fearful of death. I just could not accept the possibility that my personality would be gone forever when I pass on. One day my jaw suddenly locked on me. It was frozen in place, and I was scared to death. My parents, in a panic, called our family physician and explained the problem to him. The doctor called our pharmacy and ordered one Librium capsule for me. Librium is a minor tranquilizer. I took the pill and within a minute or two my jaw was fine. Obviously the pill was not the cause of the relief. When working with patients suffering panic attacks I would make use of this placebo effect. I would first teach patients exactly what is going on in their bodies when they are experiencing a panic attack. I would then teach them strategies to minimize the symptoms. This was sufficient with some of the patients. With others I would take it a step further. I would ask them to have their physician prescribe a minor tranquilizer that they should keep handy. Women I would tell to keep the medication in their pocketbook or purse. Next I would tell them "If the strategies I have taught you aren't sufficient to stop the panic attacks then, and only then, will you take the pill. If you take the pill only on rare occasions it will work like magic."

Suggestion provided by a respected medical source is powerful. A fair number of the patients I had so treated never ended up taking any tranquilizer at all. Just knowing that it was available as a safety net was enough. I call this the security blanket effect. The exceptions were the patients who were seeing a psychiatrist and were already taking medication on a schedule for a period of time. These patients had been convinced that they needed the medicine since the panic attacks were biological in origin. These patients were by far the hardest to treat. The field of psychiatry made an absolutely horrendous mistake when it restricted practice to solely prescribing medication. In my opinion the mistake has stopped many people from getting the help they need and needs to be openly discussed and corrected.

Getting back to Larry Dossey. In the mid 1950's it was found that placebo's (so called sugar pills) could have effects as good or almost as good as actual medications. The influence of the mind on the body could no longer be doubted. The age of mind-body medicine came about. Experimental psychologists would go on to show that animals placed under stress developed physical problems, and eventually medical researchers would show that humans undergoing prolonged stress not only developed hypertension but a whole host of other medical disorders as well. We now know that prolonged stress cannot only make you ill, but will hinder your immune systems ability to heal you. The same can be said for clinical depression.

Today we are witnessing the birth of era three medicine. Due to the entrenched materialistic views held in medicine era three medicine will grow very slowly. Remember that Vitamin C was recommended to prevent scurvy in sailors, but it took a few hundred years after the recommendation made by Dr. James Lin before the medical association finally accepted this. Likewise era three medicine will take time, but it too will eventually be accepted.

Era three medicine was brought about by two of the findings from the new paradigm of science. The first of these findings is non-locality or the fact that things can influence other things without coming into direct contact with them. The billiard ball universe of Newton no longer holds.

According to Dossey, the hallmark of era three medicine he terms non-local mind, or the rediscovery of the ancient realization that the consciousness can free itself from the body and act non-locally on distant people, animals, plants and also inanimate objects. This is supported by findings such as those of Robert Jahn and associates at Princeton University. They showed us that people could focus their minds on random number generators and alter the printout from the machines. If our minds can alter inanimate objects imagine how much more we can influence people with whom we are entangled.

Entanglement is the second finding from the new physics that has tremendous implications for healthcare. Once again Jahn's studies come into play. Strangers working together can influence an inanimate object (computer generated random line). If you allow the strangers to interact for an hour prior to the experiment they then have greater influence on the random line. Husbands and wives with strong relationships influence the randomly generated line the most. Scientifically this is not surprising since photons that had come into contact for a period of time become entangled and afterwards can influence the behavior of their partner. Jahn showed us that humans also have this ability. The more bonded or entangled people become the greater the influence they can have on inanimate objects and we shall soon see also on each other. My own theory is that today's computer age has so constantly bombarded us with stimuli that it has interfered with relational entanglement (the technical term is called decoherance) and led to a greater alienation and disenchantment among society. This does not bode well for future generations.

In effect era three medicine is the ability of individuals or groups to use their minds to influence an outcome in an individual who is ill. For as long as I can remember we have been told to pray for the sick. I know I had doubted the ability of my prayers to influence a physically based medical condition in the past, but no longer. I will now present some of the research that has led to my own personally changed beliefs.

I will begin with research performed by Dean Radin and colleagues. Once again Radin's book *"Entangled Mind"* is a treasure chest of such studies.

Radin conducted a study in which thirty-six couples were evaluated to see if their emotional bonds translated into physical ones. During the study each partner in a couple was placed in a separate room. The rooms were shielded so that each person was not able to see, talk or communicate in any way with his or her partner. Both individuals were wired so that a computer could record various physiological measurements such as heart rate, respiration, brain wave activity, skin conductance and peripheral blood flow. These are all measures of a person's autonomic or unconscious nervous system.

For thirty minutes one partner would send ten second bursts of focused loving intentions to the other at random times. A computer measured each partner's nervous system. The question to be studied was "does the senders transmissions impact the other partners nervous system? " Radin had hypothesized that long-term couples will be entangled both emotionally and physically. This bears similarity to the Princeton studies already mentioned in which long-term couples influenced the randomly generated line the most. Further, Radin hypothesized that he would receive the greatest results from couples where one partner was sick. Radin believed that such couples would be especially sensitive to each other.

When Radin and his partner Schlitz analyzed the results of all thirty-six couples in the study they found that when one person "sent" his or her compassionate intention to his or her partner the partners physiology reacted within two seconds. The correlations were high. The odds of getting the results by chance were 11,000 to one for all the bonded couples, and when you looked at the highly motivated couples, the ones facing cancer, the odds were even much higher 135,000 to one.

In the book *"Fingerprints of God"* author Barbara Hagerty discusses a study performed by Jeanne Achtenberg, a psychology professor at Saybrook Institute in San Francisco. Jeanne and her colleagues gathered together eleven Shaman healers on the big island of Hawaii. At random intervals each healer prayed for a close friend as the friend lay in a brain scanner. When Achtenberg analyzed the brain scans she was astonished by the results. During the intervals when the healers were sending their prayers and intentions, the partner's brains "lit up". The brains lit up in areas that are usually associated with response to a stimulus. Achtenberg theorized that the stimulus was the healer's thoughts. The odds against this finding by chance were 7,874 to one.

Along this line of research, Radin mentions that in 2003 Leanne Standish and her colleagues at Bastyr University performed the following experiment: Participants were put into FMRI machines. A flashing light stimulated the visual cortex of one participant's brain. At the very same moment her partner in a distant FMRI machine displayed stimulation in the same area of the brain. Once again the odds against chance were found to be highly significant.

As could be predicted Dean Radin mentions that the very strongest findings of all come when identical twins are placed in MRI machines. I would have assumed this as the twins come from one egg and have shared the same womb for nine months. Identical twins are truly entangled, and all sorts of studies show this.

These and other studies prove that thoughts can be transmitted across space to influence another individual. This further proves that the cause and effect billiard ball universe of Newton is now a part of history. Somehow not only photons but humans as well have the ability to communicate non-locally.

At this point in time many well respected universities and research centers are investigating the power of prayer to help in healing the sick. Findings are not always consistent. The main reason for this is the difficulty performing research on humans. When we separate groups of patients into one group being prayed for and the other not being prayed for we run into a problem. The reasoning should be quite obvious. How can we stop the family and friends from not praying for the patients in the no prayer control group?

It is for this reason that many researchers chose to perform studies on mice, seeds and bacteria. With the exception of Mickey and Minnie Mouse I doubt that many mice were praying for other mice. I definitely know that the seeds and bacteria weren't doing so. These studies avoided almost all of the problems inherent in research on humans, and provide strong evidence for the power of prayer.

PRAYER AND THE SICK

Next I examined some of the studies purporting to demonstrate the power of prayer to heal the sick. Most books I have read begin by stating the pioneering study of Dr. Randolph Byrd. Dr. Byrd was a heart specialist working in San Francisco General Hospital. Dr. Byrd used as subjects close to four hundred patients who had been admitted to the cardiac intensive-care unit. Patients were divided into two groups. No one knew which group they were assigned to. Not only the patients but the physicians themselves were kept blind as to group assignment. One group of patients were prayed for by religious groups that had been given the patients first names and some information regarding their medical condition. The other group received only traditional medical care. Family and friends were not told to stop praying for the second group. As has been noted this is the difficulty with such research. At the end of the study Dr. Byrd found that the prayed for group did much better than the control group on a number of factors. The prayed for group was statistically less likely to develop congestive heart failure, pulmonary edema, being placed on respirators or requiring artificial respiration. Further it was much less likely for the prayed for group to require antibiotics or develop pneumonia. Byrd's study was the beginning of using the scientific method to evaluate the benefits of prayer on healing.

Another research study was performed by Elizabeth Targ and Fred Sicher. Elizabeth was the daughter of Russell Targ from remote viewing fame. Unfortunately this very bright, educated woman passed away at an early age. Life is a gift not to be wasted. In his book "*Limitless Mind*" Russell Targ describes his daughter's pioneering research. The research was carried out at California Pacific Medical Center. Subjects for the studies were men with advanced AIDS. The research hypothesized that an intensive ten-week distant healing intervention by experienced healers located around the United States would benefit the medical outcomes for a population of advanced AIDS patients in the San Francisco Bay Area. According to Russell Targ two separate randomized double blind studies were performed. In the first twenty men were paired by number of AIDS defining illnesses. In the second forty men were carefully matched by age, T-cell count and number of AIDS defining illnesses. The patient's medical conditions were assessed after the distant healing intervention, and again six months later.

In the first study four of the ten control subjects died, while all of the patients in the treatment group survived. Unequal age distribution between the two groups may have played a role in the findings and therefore the second study was much more carefully designed to rule out such a possibility.

Regarding the healers, forty people took part. They were from Christian, Jewish, Buddhist, Native American and Shamanic Traditions. All had had at least five years of experience with distant prayer. Healers rotated patients they prayed for, and prayed one hour a day for six days a week. They were instructed to pray for the health and well being of their patients. By the end of the study it was clear that the prayed for patients experienced significantly improved quality of life. Elizabeth concluded that decreased hospital visits, fewer new severe diseases and greatly improved health supports the hypothesis of the positive therapeutic effects of distant healing.

A study reported in the September 2001 issue of the Journal of Reproductive Medicine I found even more surprising. With what we have now learned regarding entanglement I can somewhat understand the positive impact prayer can have on a patients immune system, but this study went beyond that.

The study involved in vitro fertilization. Rogerio Lobo M.D chairman of the Department of Obstetrics and Gynecology at Columbia University College of Physicians and Surgeons was lead investigator. The study, which had several safeguards in place to eliminate bias, involved 199 women planning in vitro fertilization and embryo transfers at the Cha Hospital in Seoul, Korea, between December 1998 and March 1999. The researchers randomly assigned the prospective mothers to either a prayer group (100 women) or a non-prayer group (99 women). Besides the women not knowing which group they were assigned to the physicians and medical personnel caring for the women did not know that a study of prayer effectiveness was occurring.

The people praying lived in the United States, Canada, and Australia and were incapable of knowing or contacting the women undergoing the procedures. The people praying were from Christian denominations and were separated into three groups. One group received pictures of the women and prayed for an increase in their pregnancy rate. Another group prayed to improve the effectiveness of the first group's fertilization. A third group prayed for the other two groups. I had never heard of such a procedure but the researchers reported that anecdotal evidence from other prayer research had found this method to be effective. The three groups began to pray within five days of the initial hormone treatment and continued to pray for three weeks.

Now we get to the results. The women prayed for had a fifty percent rate of pregnancy while the non-prayed for women had only a twenty six percent rate of pregnancy. The findings were even a little higher when older women were analyzed separately.

Kwang Y. Cha M.D, director of the Cha Hospital and an associate research scientist at OB/GYN at Columbia University College of Physicians and Surgeons funded the research through his hospital, and his colleagues helped to carefully design the study to avoid any alternative explanations for the findings.

THE POWER OF FAITH

While prayer has been found to have a positive impact on healing and even in vitro pregnancies I believe there is a second factor that influences healing even more. That factor is the spiritual belief of the individual ill and also the individual praying for that person. For this I turn to research into Native American healing. Such healing, and similar healing by Shamans and their brethren around the world may not have been tested scientifically as of yet, but regardless the individual case studies especially when taken in the context of the information I have already provided are extremely compelling. For those interested in looking into this I recommend the book "*Coyote Medicine*" by Lewis Medrona M.D.

Medrona is an interesting study in and on himself. He calls himself a half-breed since he is part Native American. Always fascinated by Native American healing he took every opportunity to study with healers. At the same time he was also studying traditional medicine. Medrona ran into problems because he was outspoken and wouldn't keep still during his residencies when he saw wrongful traditional medicine being practiced. For example, Medrona tells of an obstetrician trying to break the time record for performing a caesarean birthing. The doctor broke the record but in his rush he made a mistake and the mother almost bled to death. Medrona saw other obstetricians performing caesareans needlessly because they wanted to finish before office hours. Due to his outspoken behavior he was forced to resign from two residencies. Despite his trials and tribulations Medrona stuck to his beliefs and now successfully combines the best of both traditional and Native American healing. I am writing about Medrona because he has a point that we all need to hear. That point is this:" *Relying solely on rational, materialistic explanations is destroying medicine."* Medrona argues, and I certainly agree, that to be healed we need to believe strongly in the possibility of healing and should not trivialize the power of spiritual belief. Dr. Medrona takes us into a Native American healing ceremony. Analyzing it I see that it involves several stages completed over several days. In the first the patient's body is cleansed in a sweat lodge and also through fasting. In the second stage the patient is introduced to the spiritual beliefs of Native Americans. In the final stage an alternative reality is created by the setting (drums, chanting, prayers, and some times even a dose of peyote). Medrona believes the result depends on the degree of belief that has been established. When the person to be healed accepts the spiritual beliefs, and their power to heal, amazing improvements can be had. In his book Medrona talks about serious illnesses that could not be healed by traditional medicine. Dossey, Morse, Medrona and other medical doctors I have read all tell stories of miraculous healings occurring in every hospital. I will always remember that during my own postdoctoral training in psychopharmacology we were told of one man who was given less than one month to live from stage four cancer that had metastasized throughout his body. One day the man signed himself out of the hospital. He then booked a hotel and spent every day watching reruns of the Three Stooges, Abbott and Costello and Groucho Marx. He had read of the power of laughter. For one month he laughed and laughed. At the end of the month he went back to the hospital. He was found to be in complete remission. How is this possible? If one relies solely on traditional medicine it can't be explained.

In his book *"Spiritual Healing"* psychiatrist Daniel Benor describes over one hundred studies of spiritual healing. Some of the patients studied had what could be said to be miraculous healings.

As has already been discussed the studies performed on animals and plants are routinely positive. The studies on human subjects tend to be mixed. Some are significant while others are inconclusive. With human studies there can be too many confounding effects.

Regarding the implications for the new science on healthcare we have learned that psychic energy can somehow, though not yet fully understood, be transmitted from one person to another. From studies on entanglement we know that the more entangled people become the greater the influence they can have. We also know that traditional medicine is literally stuck in a materialistic model where consciousness is localized in the brain and can be influenced solely by physical (chemical) means. The time is ripe to question the old model and initiate change. Fortunately there are those at the forefront of this changing of the guard.

COMPASSION AND HEALTHCARE

In 1988 Arnold and Sandra Gold and their medical colleagues at Columbia Universities College of Physicians and Surgeons established a foundation. The goal of the Arnold P. Gold Foundation is to instill a culture of respect, dignity and compassion for patients and professionals. Their motto is "Humanistic healthcare is not simply compassion it is the best of medicine." The Foundation provides grants to researchers carrying out studies testing the hypothesis that compassionate healthcare is superior to traditional healthcare. Helen Reiss M.D. is the Director of the "Empathy and Relational Science Program" at Massachusetts General Hospital and an Associate Professor at Harvard Medical School. Her program has conducted many such studies. Basically what they have done is to compare traditional medical care to care by physicians and nurses who have been trained in communication skills and establishing rapport with patients. Across the board they have found that treatment by empathetic physicians is superior to the treatment by physicians following standard practice. Many of the studies performed followed scientific double blind procedures and findings routinely favored the enhanced communication over the standard treatment. Not only did they find improvements on factors such as weight loss, blood pressure, blood sugar, lipid levels and pain, but the common cold was cured faster, and surprisingly they found their results were better than taking low dose aspirin for avoiding heart attacks and comparable to taking statins for lowering heart attack risk.

For years we have known that when a doctor is empathetic and compassionate patients are more likely to follow medical advice, but now we know that there is hard physical evidence of the benefits of empathetic and compassionate doctors.

I'M A NEW MAN

While I began exploring physics, and especially the new paradigm of physics, as a way of overcoming remaining cognitive issues from my stroke an unexpected event occurred. I came to realize that the issues many people have with religion and God were not Bible issues but rather man made issues. The Bible never said that the Earth was the center of the universe, or told us the age of the planet. It was men who said these things. In actuality the Bible was correct about several things that scientists had mistaken. The Bible offers wisdom that is sorely needed in our trying times, and so my wife and I joined a Bible church. I had never before met such really nice people. When I listened to testimonies from pastors and members I realized that they were very much like me, and like me, had found God.

My wife and I began volunteering in two food pantries: one pantry for the community, and one for our church. Further our old church was part of a network that took homeless families in every sixth week. The families arrived at dinner-time and slept overnight. I began cooking on weekends for the families. An acquaintance told me I would never work for no pay. I responded then you would never know what you are missing. Giving back was a blessing that made me feel good inside, and doing it together with my wife strengthened our already strong relationship.

INTEGRATING SPIRITUALITY INTO PSYCHOTHERAPY

Hopefully I have opened your mind to the new paradigm being created in science and the implications it has for healthcare and for incorporating spirituality into treatment. I would now like to take a moment and discuss how I incorporated this into my private practice the last half-dozen years prior to my retirement. I will do so by means of several case studies.

Sam was a 40-year-old pharmacist. He owned his own pharmacy. It was just Sam and a clerk. One day a man walked in, pointed a gun, and said give me the cash and pills. Sam told his clerk to give the cash. The man then asked for Oxycodone, Vicodin and Xanax. Sam collected the drugs and brought them to the counter. The gunman said this is all? You must have more. Sam told him his is a small pharmacy. The gunman called Sam a liar and smashed him on the forehead with the butt of his gun. A few weeks later I received a phone call from a neurologist friend. He was referring Sam to me for treatment of PTSD. Sam was a short man and had a bald spot on the back of his head. He described how he could not get the incident out of his mind. Sam told me he wasn't sleeping, and if he should fall asleep he had nightmares of being harmed. I saw Sam twice weekly for four weeks. We worked on desensitizing him to the PTSD. While he was out of work he had hired a retired pharmacist to cover for him. At the end of the fourth week Sam felt ready to return to work, but told me he enjoyed our sessions, and there was something not related to the incident that he would like my help with.

Sam blamed it all on his critical father. He had a huge fear of being rejected and so had rarely dated. Sam was fixed up by friends and family, but was so nervous that he sabotaged himself by not calling girls back for future dates. The day he turned 40 Sam said was the worst day of his life. He badly wanted to be married and have children but was afraid that he had waited too long. Once he began thinking this way depression set in. During sessions I learned that Sam, like his father, was an atheist. He attended temple with his mother on High Holy Days out of a sense of obligation. We began to discuss the fact that people who do attend church or temple on a regular basis have been found to be happier and more well adjusted individuals than people who don't. Sam was a scientist. He enjoyed learning the new research I began sharing with him. I told him I do not agree with everything the church is saying, but research has proven to me that we do have a creator and consciousness does survive death. Also that prayer does help healing. I mentioned that what he had been doing for 40 years hasn't worked out too well for him and now is the time to give something new a try. Sam hired the retired pharmacist for Saturday's. He himself began attending temple. I noticed a change after a few weeks. Sam even joined a Kabbalah study class. He is a friendly man and quickly made friends. One evening he went, with my encouragement, to a Jewish singles dance. There he met Ellen. Ellen was a thirty-five year old teacher. After their first date he was nervous about calling her back. I told him if you trust me at all you would tell her of your fear of rejection. I guarantee she has the same fears. I absolutely guarantee it, and when you share your fear it will only serve to strengthen your relationship. He did, and it did. Two months later he asked her to marry him. He came in to our next session with a huge smile. He did tell me that between work and Ellen he didn't have time for therapy. He also said he really didn't need it as he was no longer depressed. I shook his hand and congratulated him.

From graduate school I had gotten the impression that religion was not a topic that you spent time discussing. How wrong they were.

Shoshana was a bright 19 year old girl. Shoshana was an only child, and had just begun her first term at Brooklyn College. Shortly after beginning school her life was altered drastically. Shoshana's father was a member of the Army Reserves and was in Afghanistan. While riding in a Humvee, escorting a general to a meeting, the Humvee hit a roadside bomb. Two of the accompanying soldiers were killed. The general and her father survived. The father did sustain serious head injuries as well as multiple orthopedic injuries. He was flown to a hospital in Germany, and eventually to Walter Reed Hospital in the United States. When Shoshana saw her father in the hospital wrapped in bandages, with tubes coming out of his body, and unable to utter more than sounds she was visibly shaken. The wife was told that her husband would survive but would require years of rehabilitation, and may never be able to walk. Over the next couple of months her mother, who was not a strong individual, began to drink. Shoshana found her life turned upside down. She had trouble eating and sleeping, and had trouble concentrating on her schoolwork. The mother ended up bringing Shoshana to a psychiatrist. An anti-depressant (Zoloft) was prescribed. About one month after starting the medication Shoshana started having negative dreams. These were followed by suicidal thoughts. Eventually she told her mother. The mother got my name from her insurance company. The first thing I did was to call the psychiatrist. He weaned her off of the medication, and wanted her to start another anti-depressant. After her experience with Zoloft she did not wish any medication.

My first impression, upon meeting Shoshana, was that she was so sad. She looked to me like she was lost and was having trouble coping with the serious changes to her life. On the positive side she was a bright and inquisitive young lady. By the time of our first meeting I had included in my waiting room articles showing the power of prayer, and discussing the latest paranormal research. Shoshana began coming in fifteen minutes earlier than her appointment to read the articles. During sessions she began asking me questions about them. Everyone needs hope and she saw in the articles possibilities. One of the first things I did was to give her my copy of *"The Brain That Changes Itself."* This book gave detailed accounts of people who had suffered massive strokes and within a year or two were back at work and functioning well. Strategies to help overcome brain injuries were included throughout. As my own stroke symptoms were mostly cognitive this book led to my studying physics as a way of forming new neural nets and helping myself overcome cognitive issues. Everyone recovering from a stroke should read this book. Shoshana hated to see her father in a wheelchair. *"He was always so active his whole life, and this is killing him."* I spoke to Shoshana about getting her family and friends to pray daily for her father to be able to walk again. *"There is so much research supporting this why not give it a chance."* She did and included her friends in her prayer list.

As time went on she began looking more hopeful. She now had a plan for helping her father. She began eating and sleeping better and her schoolwork began improving. Shoshana turned out to be an "A" student at learning meditation and deep relaxation with guided imagery. No longer did she suffer the occasional panic attacks that resulted from her feeling of helplessness.

The mother was pleased with her daughter's progress, and asked if she herself could be seen. I referred the mother to a female therapist in my office. During one of my last sessions with Shoshana the father came in. He walked with the help of one three pronged cane and one regular cane, but had a smile on his face upon meeting, and thanked me for all the help I had given him and his family.

The pill has not yet been invented to teach a person how to overcome serious life problems. Human compassion and counsel is the answer.

The next case is that of Susan. Susan was a 50-year-old woman suffering obsessive-compulsive disorder with panic attacks. This is a debilitating mental illness that can restrict patients lives terribly. For years Susan had been treated by a psychiatrist who currently was prescribing her an antidepressant (Paxil 40 mg's) as well as a minor tranquilizer (Xanax 1 mg). The Xanax she was taking three times a day.

Susan told me that the medication does help but her problems are as bad as ever. In addition to seeing a psychiatrist she had seen several psychotherapists throughout the years.

From my years of experience fears such as hers usually get their start from a fear of death. I began by questioning her about her childhood. It turns out that her grandmother had died when she was 6 years old. This was her first experience with death and when her parents took her to the funeral parlor she was so scared. At around age 8 she remembered becoming very angry at her parents one day. She wished them both to die. This is not that uncommon in childhood, but in her case it almost came true. One month after she had this wish her father had a major heart attack. He came close to dying. Susan blamed herself. She attributed the heart attack to her thoughts regarding her parents dying. Fear of her own thoughts became instilled in her, and has remained so until this day. Susan told me of how when she was in her late teens she would cut herself when she had bad thoughts regarding someone. Cutting is something I saw so much of when I had worked at Wingate high school. The cutting is a way to temporarily reduce anxiety. Fortunately Susan was scared of blood and discontinued this behavior. Instead she would berate herself whenever she had bad thoughts. For a while she would punish herself by engaging in tasks, she found disgusting, such as cleaning the toilet. Apparently her family doctor recommended this after reading a journal article. Monitoring of her thoughts had long been an obsession for Susan.

Now in graduate school they taught us that a psychologist should avoid sharing personal information with patients. The reason for this was so as not to hinder the transference. This is a psychoanalytic concept, and most of my teachers had graduated from psychoanalytic training institutes. There were a few patients that I did avoid sharing personal information with, but with most of my patients, and especially after my new learning, I believe that sharing can strengthen the therapeutic relationship and prove to be a teaching moment. I explained to Susan how, after my grandmother died and I became fearful of death, I began saying my prayers multiple times each night to make sure that I had gotten them perfectly said. I explained how children sometimes believe that their thoughts can influence outcomes such as death of loved ones.

I went on to explain to her how I had overcome this, but since it had been going on for so long in her case she needed help to overcome her fears. Like with Shoshana, and other patients, I explained to her all the new research regarding prayer, and then told her that my wife and I attend a Calvary Church in New Jersey that is large and has a number of ministry's that deal with issues such as overcoming fear and also guilt for past behaviors. I told her how the support and fellowship is cathartic. I mentioned that when I joined volleyball I was required to share my testimony. I considered myself pretty bad during my teens and early twenties. The other players were so supportive, and I eventually found out from listening to other testimonies that my experiences were not that uncommon, and my behaviors weren't so bad after all.

Susan, who like many Christians, attended church sporadically. She found a church in her neighborhood that offered groups that focused on forgiving oneself. Her group motto was *"If Jesus can forgive you why can't you forgive yourself."* A few months after beginning she told me that she was no longer monitoring her thoughts as much anymore and her anxieties were even less than before. She felt she could beat her problem. As an added benefit she had made nice friends, and found out that they had fears as well.

And then there is the case of Sandra. Sandra was a 19-year-old young woman. She had received her drivers license within one week of turning 18. Sandra had recently begun her sophomore year at Long Island University located in downtown Brooklyn. One evening she was driving her twin brother Carl to meet their parents at her aunt's house in Queens. While driving a deer suddenly ran out in front of her car. Sandra hit her brakes hard, and the car swerved. She went off the road and hit a tree at about 50 miles an hour. She received bruises, but her brother was killed in the crash. Sandra was distraught. She blamed herself for her brothers' death. Sandra had much trouble concentrating on her schoolwork, suffered terrible nightmares, and was overwhelmed with guilt. The parents knew she needed professional help. Their insurance company gave them my name. For several months I concentrated on desensitizing Sandra to her feelings of guilt. Progress was slow but steady. I knew that developing a compassionate therapeutic relationship would be key in her case. One day she suddenly mentioned that one of her friends had been trying for some time to convince her to see a psychic. Her friend swore by this person. She told Sandra that when she had gone to the psychic the person knew things about her boyfriend that no one could have possibly known. It was as if the psychic had hired private investigators to learn all about his life.

Sandra went on to tell me that for quite awhile now she had been hearing noises in her closet at bedtime. Whenever she checks in the morning there is nothing there. She then mentioned that a few weeks before she entered her room to find there was a lamp lit. Her parents were not at home, and she was positive that she had not lit the lamp. The articles in my waiting room had gotten her wondering.

Sandra asked what I thought of psychics. I told her that I believed at least 90% were outright frauds, but enough scientific research had now been done to prove that some people clearly have a gift. As a matter of fact there is literature that describes people who clearly had that gift in past centuries.

Sandra went to see her friend's psychic. When next we met she talked nonstop about her meeting. The psychic had told her things about her brother that no one could have known. She said she did this to prove to Sandra that she was in contact with her brother. She then told Sandra that she wanted her to believe because her brother had a message for her. He had been trying to gain her attention for quite sometime now. *The psychic told Sandra: "Your brother loves you so much and does not blame you for his death. He is watching over you and wants you to be happy in life. He himself is in a wonderful place surrounded by love. Someday you will be together again but not now."*

Following her session with the psychic our sessions quickly changed. Sandra became a different person. She was determined to make the most of her life. Her sleeping was better. Her nightmares were gone, and her schoolwork was much improved. Was this real? I do not know. What I do know is that she was helped greatly by the comfort she received from the psychic.

For twenty-seven years of my practice I cannot remember any patient telling me of a paranormal experience they had had. Everything changed once I began discussing the latest scientific research into prayer etc. Patients told me they were afraid to tell me because they thought I might think they were crazy. It turns out that about 2/3 of my female patients and 1/3 of my male patients told of having a paranormal experience in their lives. Many of these experiences seem to have happened within the first year of a loved ones death. Listening to these and similar stories made me reevaluate the way I had been practicing. I asked questions I never would have before.

The final case I will present has to do with a grieving widow. Grieving for a loved ones loss is the area that I believe adding a spiritual component can be most helpful to patients.

Mary was a deeply depressed 65-year-old woman. She had been married to her high school sweetheart for 46 years. She had just turned 19 and John 21 when they married. It was a Saturday afternoon, and John was weeding his garden. The garden was his pride and joy. When he did not come in for lunch she called to him, but got no response. Mary started to become concerned. She left the house and walked to the garden. Mary found her husband lying face down among the tomato plants. He had suffered a massive heart attack. A neighbor heard her screams and called 911. It was too late. John was dead by the time help arrived.

Mary and John had five grown children. All but one lived outside her state. They all immediately came to her side. When I did become involved, I found out that the husband and wife had been each other's best friend from high school. They were said to be inseparable throughout their marriage. Friends and family members tried hard to console Mary but she became more and more depressed. Eventually she was referred to a psychiatrist. The psychiatrist had a psychologist within his office to provide psychotherapy. The psychologist worked with Mary utilizing a cognitive behavioral format. Months passed and Mary was not improving. Instead she began having physical symptoms. Her arthritis was worsening. She had previously had a mild case of Scoliosis, but now began developing a hump in her back, and began walking bent over. She had pain shooting down her leg. It is not at all uncommon for people who have lost a spouse of many years to begin suffering physical symptoms. Statistics show that the surviving spouse will often evidence a serious medical condition within two years of their spouse dying. Today we know that this is due to the fact of the mind-body connection. Both depression and prolonged stress can undermine the functioning of the immune system as well as individual cells.

Approximately one year after her husband's death a friend of Mary had heard, from her friend, of a talk I had given at a church. Mary came to see me. She told me that both her psychiatrist and psychologist were from Russia, and were atheists. She needed something more. Her and her husband were Christians, went weekly to Bible study, and believed deeply in Christ. Her friend had told her that I was a psychologist who believed in the power of spiritual belief to help with healing. I put together a plan to help her. During sessions I discussed the research that supported consciousness surviving death, and how there were now so many documented stories of people having near death experiences being met by their loved ones in Heaven. At the end of each session I gave her reading homework to do

There are so many positive books available at this time. Next, since I have training as a clinical hypnotherapist I would put her in a light trance and get across the following suggestions:

This life is but a grain of sand on an infinitely large beach.
This life is Gods way of strengthening our soul.

John loved you so much and wouldn't want to see you suffering.
You and John will be together again.

As she began to evidence progress I encouraged her to get involved in helping other widows cope with their grief. She joined a grieving group at her church and became a co-leader. Mary developed a more positive attitude and felt she had a purpose now. The look in her eyes said it all. By the way she went back to caring for her husbands garden.

When I began my practice I was a cognitive behavioral psychotherapist. Cognitive theory tells us that irrational thinking, often learned in childhood, leads to irrational behaviors. The job of the psychotherapist is to identify the irrational thoughts underlying the behaviors and then help the patient alter these for more functional thoughts. One example is the men who are so afraid of asking a woman out due to irrational fear of rejection. I did have several patients like this. I explained earlier how Albert Ellis had overcome his own fears through a behavioral program.

I came to realize however that patients often needed help on more than just this level. In the last several years of my practice I changed. I became a mind-body-spiritual psychotherapist. I recognized that for true healing to occur all three aspects of a person must be considered.

Irrational thoughts must be corrected. Exercise and proper nutrition is helpful, and we must avoid the mistake that society is making with over concern with materialistic things and recognize the importance of seeing ourselves as spiritual beings. I had gone from a person who had little to do with religion to one who now believed strongly that this earthly life is but a tiny grain of sand on an infinitely large beach.

HEALTHCARE RECOMMENDATIONS

As I look at the state of healthcare around the country I see many positive changes. Some of the most impressive are happening in cancer care centers. Cancer care centers are now incorporating alternative therapies to humanize treatment. Patients are trained to meditate. They are given massage, and are seen by nutritionists. Social workers and psychologists are there to help patients cope with life stress, and chaplains are available to pray with patients. Treatment in cancer care centers is now focused on the entire person and as a result success rates are climbing.

Larry Dossey, in his implications for healthcare, indicates when discussing the era three emergency room that prayer groups be added and notified to begin praying for seriously ill patients. Now that we know that prayer can help mice heal from incisions made into their backs, seeds to grow better, healing intentions to be received by individuals lying in FMRI machines, and AIDS and cardiac patients to have fewer medical complications it is time to recognize the healing effects of prayer much more urgently.

Just as the remote viewers were trained to use their minds to see things going on in foreign countries or into containers aboard ships I suggest that healers can be trained to focus their minds on improving medical conditions. There are already countless stories of individual healers. One such story that stood out for me was described by Ervin Laszlo in his book *"Science and the Akashic Field."* In the presence of the author and about one hundred seminar participants Dr. Guntar Hadfelder, head of the Institute for Brain Research of Stuttgart, Germany, measured the EEG patterns of Dr. Maria Sagi, a trained psychologist and gifted natural healer, together with the EEG patterns of a young man who volunteered from among the participants. The young man remained in the seminar hall while the healer was taken to a separate room. Both the healer and the young man were wired with electrodes, and their EEG patterns were projected on a large screen in the hall. The healer diagnosed the health problems of the subject, while he sat with closed eyes in a light meditative state. When the healer had correctly identified the subject's areas of organic dysfunction, she sent instructions designed to compensate for them. During the approximately fifteen minutes that the healer was concentrating on her task, her EEG waves dipped into the deep Delta region with a few sudden eruptions of wave amplitude. This was surprising in itself, because when someone's brain waves descend into the Delta region, he or she is usually in a state of deep sleep. The healer though was fully awake, in a state of deep concentration. Even more surprising was that the test subject exhibited the same Delta wave pattern. The pattern showed up in his EEG display about two seconds after it appeared in the EEG of the healer. As in other studies already reported this occurred even though the two had had no sensory contact. There are numerous such studies of healers correctly diagnosing and recommending treatment for people who are ill. So far as I know Edgar Cayce remains the undisputed champion.

What I am going to suggest is a new medical field of study that is based on the findings of current research.

For interested medical and psychological researchers I recommend the following. First, new healers spend time bonding. Participating in group counseling during my second year of graduate school was very positive for strengthening the bonds among students. Further, Jahn's research showed us that strangers who spent time getting to know each other prior to the experimental situation had a greater effect then if they hadn't spent this time together. Second, new healers should be trained to focus their minds intently as the remote viewers were trained to do. Anyone who has tried to meditate knows all about those fleeting, competing thoughts. Meditation takes time to learn. Third, new healers must study the research literature on the power of prayer, suggestion, and faith, as all have shown a positive effect on illness. Only then after much practice with animals and plants, the new healers can be assigned to send healing intentions to patients suffering illnesses such as cancer or AIDS. With cancer I would suggest spending about twenty to thirty minutes each day sending the intention of immune cells being sent to destroy tumors. With AIDS patients I suggest sending the healing intention of strengthening immune cell responses. I realize what I am suggesting is evaluating the feasibility of establishing a new profession within the medical community. Now I know that there are plenty of people out there who will think my idea is pie in the sky and utter fantasy. What they don't realize is that for much of the world this has been the healthcare they are used to. In eastern cultures knowledge of proper nutrition, herbs and alternative healthcare is also a must.

It is in this last subject area that the United States healthcare system falls short. The government keeps complaining of the inflationary cost in healthcare, but develops programs that will only increase costs. I have spoken with literally one hundred physicians about the solution to healthcare costs and the answer is always the same. Instead of treating people only after they get sick we need to focus intently on preventative healthcare. It turns out that the costliest health issues are all behavioral issues. Overeating and resulting diabetes is number one. Diabetics will require expensive treatments and can live near normal life spans. They even have to go to podiatrists just to have their toenails cut. Smoking is second, followed by drug and alcohol abuse and finally promiscuous sex without condoms. If we are going to reduce the cost of healthcare we need to have a carefully planned educational war on all of these. Unfortunately only smoking has seen such a campaign. The rest are merely given lip service.

When the government does come up with ideas for improvements they tend not to work. For example the war on drugs only created cartels that have terrorized whole countries and drug gangs that have terrorized inner cities. You would think politicians learned their lesson from prohibition. From day one the drug war should have been an educational and medical one. Unfortunately the bureaucracy is well established and like any entrenched bureaucracy will be difficult to alter. I must give one example of the idiocy of government policy. Due to my specialty I saw patients taking opiate medications for pain. They mostly receive the medicine from pain specialists. The doctors are required to take random urine tests two or three times each year to make sure that the patients are really taking the medicine and not selling it. As the testing only occurs when the patient is seeing his or her doctor there is nothing random about it. Further, if a patient wants to beat the system all they have to do is to take the medicine for two days prior to being tested. They can then sell the rest.

The proposal of training and utilizing healers to supplement traditional healthcare, given our new knowledge of non-local communication and entanglement, and the extensive supportive research makes perfect sense. What is surprising is that western society has waited until science has given us a reason for exploring this area of healing. Eastern philosophies, on the other hand, have long accepted the unity of all things and have stressed meditation and the power of the mind to affect healing. I will long remember the story I told earlier of the master Yogi whose brain was flat-lined for an extended period of time, but his students and fellow Yogi's kept praying and praying until one day he opened his eyes and said "*It was so peaceful why did you not let me go.*" It is time for us westerners to stop doubting and start acting.

I am writing this last section in the afternoon. In the morning I spent one hour in the dentist's chair. The dentist cut down one of my teeth prepping it for a new crown, which is involved work, and also drilled a cavity in another tooth close to my gum line. As soon as I was in the chair he told his assistant to prepare the injection. I stopped him. The dentist actually pleaded with me. "*In all my years I have never done this procedure without administering an anesthetic; please it is going to be painful."* I am stubborn and wanted to prove a point. Before he began I closed my eyes and pictured myself on a beach. It was a beautiful, picture perfect day out. I slowly stepped into the water and began to swim to an island offshore. I kept my breathing slow and steady. When I felt pain I kept it in the back of my mind and just observed the flow. With each stroke I took it lessened. This idea is similar to Lamaze training and it shows the power of the mind. Pharmaceutical companies have done a great job in getting us to accept medication as the answer to all of life's problems. The new paradigm of science is leading the way to opening eyes. Medication is a last answer and not a first answer. The Medicare program is said to be going bankrupt. Focusing our system on preventative healthcare as well as alternative healthcare will go a long way to correct this situation.

WISDOM OF OUR ANCESTORS

As more and more people worldwide become comfortable with their computers, cell phones, cars and air travel, they tend to focus more on the materialistic aspects of life, and to place religion and spirituality in a back seat. There is a negative aspect to this materialistic focus. A sense of alienation is rampant and the world is becoming morally bankrupt as seen by the regional wars, mass genocide, human trafficking, crime rates, drug and alcohol abuse, nuclear proliferation etc. This is happening because we have lost our way, and ignored the wisdom of our ancestors. They placed God first and foremost.

Since the very earliest of times man had been concerned with exploring nature and trying to understand what happens when we die. Archaeologists have discovered that Neanderthal's buried their dead with ritualistic objects accompanying them. This suggests concerns with either having these objects help them achieve the afterlife or having the objects help them in the afterlife. The Egyptians took this to extreme thousands of years ago when they buried slaves, animals, and even his wife with the Pharaoh.

Cultural anthropologists had held the belief, for a long period of time, that religion did not form until man had developed an agricultural society. It was felt that once people had settled into stable communities they were then able to develop a division of labor. Eventually a priestly class came into being. Man built temples to worship gods that would protect them from the ravages of nature and also help with fertility issues.

In recent years this theory was turned on its head. Archaeologist Klaus Schmidt, a researcher at the German Archaeological Institute, in the autumn of 1994 was investigating southeastern Turkey. Nine miles outside the town where the prophet Abraham was reportedly born he came upon a hillside filled with artifacts. The area was called Gobekli Tepe. In the 1960's archaeologists from the University of Chicago had surveyed the region and determined it to be of little interest. Well it was anything but uninteresting. Klaus and his team unearthed a huge religious complex dating back 11,600 years. The area is still being excavated today. National Geographic Magazine of June, 2011 offered a huge spread on the discovery of the "world's first temple."

What is so shocking about this find? 11,600 years ago there were no agricultural communities. At that time men and women were hunters and gatherers. In small bands they roamed the countryside following the herds and picking wild tubers and fruits. They spent their day worrying about surviving until their next meal. There was no written language. There were no courses on engineering. What these people did have was a calling. They had belief. Somehow they came together and built huge complexes that dwarf Stonehenge. They used flint knives to cut out blocks of limestone weighing as much as sixteen tons. They then decorated them magnificently with bas-reliefs of vultures, scorpions and wild animals, and then somehow or other erected these huge stones to form complexes. The complexes were formed as mazes. It is thought that in different parts of the maze various ceremonies took place. The exact use of the complexes is still being debated. Think what this tells us! Years before communities were built, and while men and women were struggling daily to survive, they built the first religious complexes. It was religion and not agriculture that brought people together.

How they were able to accomplish these feats is way beyond me. I have a friend who swears that aliens helped them. I tend to hold another belief. Following the find at Gobekli Tepe numerous similar finds have been found throughout Turkey, Syria and Iraq. The point I wish to make clear is that concern with religion, spirituality, and life after death has been with us from very early on. Not only that but religious concerns were the impetus behind scientific developments. As agriculture brought people together in stable communities the discussion of topics such as the stars above, creation and nature grew. Over time the communities grew ever larger. There were no video games, cell phones, television or Facebook to distract the people. Instead with their free time they would gather and discuss issues such as life after death. Eventually the first informal philosophical schools were formed. The best known of these were in Greece.

The early Greek philosophers saw no separation between science, philosophy and religion. The term physics is coined from the Greek word physis and was concerned with discovering the essential nature of all things. Plato and Aristotle developed cosmic worldviews that incorporated a "Divine Principle" which stood above all. Eventually this "Divine Principle" would come to be seen as an intelligent and personal God who stands above the world and directs it. In time the three monotheistic religions were born and came to be practiced mostly in the West. Religion would become the prime focus of daily life for many centuries.

In the East religious philosophy took a different course. According to Capra, Buddhism, Hinduism and Taoism all emphasize the basic unity of all things. The cosmos is seen as one inseparable reality. It is forever in motion, alive, organic and spiritual and even materialistic at the same time. Physicist David Bohm's concept of an implicate and explicate order is in line with this thinking. Bohm believes that all unfolds from an implicate order which is the ultimate source of all creation. I believe the Bible would call this implicate order the Word of God. All comes about due to the creation of God.

While they have their differences all of these Eastern philosophies believe that in order to become enlightened one must learn to recognize this unity of all things and no longer allow our personal ego to see us as separate from it. The Biblical story of the eating of the Apple symbolizes this separation from God.

There can be no question that religion and spirituality, whether you were born in India or Italy, has played such a large role in the life of mankind. Not only that, but the wisdom of ancient sages should not be ignored. It was only a few decades ago that most scientists thought the universe was eternal. The Bible said there was a beginning to the universe. The Bible was correct. A few decades ago most scientists believed that the first life (single celled life) was not present on this planet for approximately the first billion years. The Bible said no. The Bible tells of life being present as soon as there was water on Earth. Again the Bible was correct. The Bible never said the earth was the center of the solar system, man did. The same can be said of the age of the earth. Misunderstandings have led to people doubting the Bible and religion.

Going even further, one of the most popular theories of everything is super string theory. Mathematicians and many physicists love super string theory because it is the first theory that brings together both Einstein's general relativity and Bohr's quantum mechanics. The worlds of the incredibly large and the incredibly small are brought together in it. Super string theory postulates ten dimensions. It so happens that the Kaballah (considered Jewish mysticism) had predicted ten dimensions many, many years ago. There are other theories in theoretical cosmology today that also predict multiple dimensions. The Kaballah beat them to the punch. The first scientists were almost all theologians.

Hindu's have spoken of the Akashic Record or universal database. The book of life is mentioned in the Bible. The concept of a universal database is finally being taken seriously today. Many believe that the military remote viewers and psychics such as Edgar Cayce tap into it. Psychologist Carl Jung spent much of his career speaking about a universal consciousness to which we can be receptive. Such a database could explain how so many things were created similarly among cultures that had never come into contact. According to Grayson It may even explain incredible stories thought to be reincarnation.

It is a mistake to reject out of hand the wisdom of our ancestors. Remember they didn't have all the distractions we have today. They spent their free time in thought and discussion. Religion and spirituality have been concerns of mankind from very early on. The fact is religion has many very positive attributes. These attributes are desperately needed today. Religions not only focus on worshipping our creator but on teaching morals and the importance of helping those in need. It literally sickened me when I heard of the Ten Commandments being removed from some public places. Atheists are behind this and similar occurrences. I believe the new paradigm of science has what is needed to begin a revival of belief. Critics of religion argue that it has led to wars. It is not religion and spirituality that causes wars and wrongdoings it is the wrongful interpretations of man. We are living through this right now. The teachings of the Koran have been horribly distorted by men wishing personal power and gain. The immense loss of life this has led to is beyond tragic, and I worry for the outcome.

SCIENCE CAN INITIATE
THE REVIVAL

Materialistic thinking has led to incredible breakthroughs in so many areas of life. But when physicists such as the eminent Lord Kelvin remarked in the late 1800's that all that remained for physics was to cross a few T's and dot a few I's he wasn't aware of what the future would hold. Man can never know everything.

Shortly after Lord Kelvin made such remarks the world of science was shattered again. It began with Einstein showing us that energy and matter was one and the same thing. There is no easier way to come to understand this then to imagine an atom bomb. The energy contained in a small bit of matter is huge and if we are not careful could spell the end of mankind. World governments **must** now focus hard on ending the proliferation of nuclear weapons. An article in Scientific American magazine (January, 2010) had estimated that if Pakistan and India went to war and released their nuclear arsenals the sun would be blocked out long enough to kill all plant life and therefore end the reign of mankind.

Shortly after Einstein's discovery came Niels Bohr and his colleagues who investigated the parts of an atom and ended up developing quantum mechanics. The founders of quantum mechanics as well as theorists even today all agree that if you say you understand quantum mechanics you have no idea what you are talking about. How can we understand particles being both a wave and also a point particle? How can we understand particles being in multiple places at the same time? How can we understand particles communicating with other particles on the other side of the galaxy? And how can we possibly comprehend particles being able to alter behaviors that have already occurred?

Physicist Lee Smolin in his book *"Time Reborn"* remarks how will we ever be able to understand consciousness when we don't know what a rock really is or an atom, or an electron. All of these are made from energy and we really do not understand energy. If we cannot understand what energy itself is think what this says for reality. The only true "reality" may be the reality of the eternal life after death. Religions may have been correct all along. It was these findings with particle physics and quantum mechanics that provided the impetus for more careful investigations into paranormal behaviors and also for philosophers to question our very notions of reality. Today major institutions worldwide are involved in studying everything from prayer, to non-local communications, near death experiences and renowned mediums. What is being found is that paranormal behaviors are much more normal than we ever realized. We have also learned that our current obsession with materialistic science has actually caused abilities that we probably had in the past to atrophy. The training required of the military remote viewers supports this. To put this another way, until we became materialistic (scientifically) our right brain was dominant and we had abilities that then atrophied due to nonuse. It is a truism: use it or lose it.

It now appears that the earliest pre-civilizations began due to religious belief and spirituality some ten thousand years ago. Religion and spirituality played a dominant role in scientific advancement for most of history as man explored the heavens and nature to help understand how we got here and where we will be going once we pass on. Science then went through a dark period due to staunch religious dogma and those who manipulated religion for personal gain. We see this today with television evangelists having large estates and private planes. Those who abused religion for personal gain, especially certain types of "gain," have seeded doubts in the minds of the public. Religion has begun to decline due to abuse by religious figures, staunch dogma, and the fact that scientific advances made life much easier for people. Some people even began to see science as a form of religion in itself. Organized religion and spirituality suffered as a result of these factors, and it has been predicted that Christianity could disappear from much of Europe in the future. We need a revival and need it now.

The new paradigm of physics has the potential to create a 180 degree-turn. Realizing that we do not truly understand reality has stopped us dead in our materialistic tracks. Our minds are limited to three- dimensional thinking and we have reason now to believe in multiple other dimensions. Scientific advances are helping us to reconsider the wisdom of our ancestors. Eastern philosophies have for thousands of years told us that "All Is One." Physicists such as the esteemed Ed. Witten of the Institute for Advanced Studies at Princeton University and many others have come to agree. Witten has argued that all that may truly exist is information. Whether it be the Akashic Field, the virtual energy of the universe or the event horizon of a massive black hole, somehow information regarding everything that has ever happened in the history of the universe appears to be stored permanently, and we are coming to see that there are people who appear able to access this. Edgar Cayce is the prime example.

Even further, science has given us reason to believe that there may be a multitude of universes possibly even infinity of universes. The biblical statement "My father's house has many rooms" can no longer be looked at the same way. Of interest to me is that more and more physicists and cosmologists are now of the opinion that there had to be a beginning, a creation, and a creation to me imply a creator. We have gone full circle and are returning to spiritual beliefs held by our ancestors. Science and spirituality are coming to see how deeply intertwined they really are.

CONCLUSION

Now is when I get to pull things together and draw conclusions. The new paradigm of physics has not only blown away classical physics, but has obliterated a materialistic conception of reality.

While it is true that materialistic science has enabled society to make incredible gains in living standards as well as lifespan, there is nevertheless a distinct downside. The downside is in people moving away from religion and spirituality. Nowhere can this be seen more clearly than in one of the world's great religions being hijacked by psychotic criminals who have no consideration for human life and indiscriminately murder people savagely. They use a grossly distorted vision of their religion to justify themselves.

Beyond this we see a world hell-bent on destruction. Governments today are spending more money on developing means of destroying people than they are on advancing life. As a result of fear, stupidity and outright greed we have nuclear proliferation, countries developing weapons from biochemical agents, human trafficking, pollution of our oceans and atmosphere, drug cartels terrorizing whole countries, and drug gangs running rampant in our inner cities. Further, due to the alienation, hedonism and materialism within society, the divorce rate is ever climbing and never before did we see so many young women having abortions. This is one thing that personally upset me greatly. While working in a high school, I saw a number of 14 and 15 year old girls who had had abortions. They were using abortions as contraception, even though the school was handing out free condoms. The girls would rather murder babies than require their boyfriends to wear them. Writing this has brought up another bad memory. While working in Wingate high school, I had just finished evaluating a nice young man with a learning disability. Shortly after the evaluation had been completed, and prior to my team meeting with the family to discuss options for his education, a terrible thing happened. One night around nine p.m. his younger sister had gone to a local store to buy milk. When she left the store she was caught in the middle of a gun battle between rival drug gangs. That young girl will never grow up to finish school and get married. Politicians so blew it. We should have learned our lesson from prohibition and the gangs created by it. As I mentioned before, from day one the war on drugs should have been an educational and medical concern. I will never forget the Rockefeller drug laws putting college students caught smoking pot in jail for ten to twenty years. Many of these students came out as hardened criminals unable to get jobs and with their lives literally destroyed. My faith in politicians is extremely poor. The upcoming Presidential election shows I am not alone.

Fortunately there is a bright sign of hope on the horizon. A multitude of groups are being established throughout the world. The focus of these groups is on spirituality and the oneness of all peoples. For centuries there have been psychical societies that included among their membership many of the greatest minds in history. Members such as William James realized that materialism was seducing us into a distorted view of reality. Great thinkers realized that the reality we see through our senses is limited and there is so much that we don't understand. Unfortunately, as materialistic science progressed more and more people ridiculed anything considered paranormal. The mindset became that if you couldn't see it or touch it then it didn't exist. The new paradigm of physics has changed that mindset forever.

All matter is created from energy and energy particles/waves obey none of the classical laws of physics. Scientists aren't even sure just what exactly energy is. The new paradigm being established has opened the doors to increased research into and respect for paranormal behaviors that were long laughed at. Today we have well designed research studies proving prayer does help, and it appears that everyone manifests some degree of paranormal ability that can be improved with training.

The most exciting research to me is the research being performed with renowned mediums. The Arizona University studies clearly show that contact with deceased individuals is a possibility. Newer studies at IONS and other institutes are consistent with their findings. When Sylvia Browne went into trance her spiritual guide Francine would speak through her. When Francine was questioned about Jesus she gave the following answer: *"Jesus is so in demand in the afterlife that he can be in a multitude of workshops at the same exact time."* Now that we know all is created from energy and energy particles can be in multiple places at the same time we can no longer just ridicule this possibility. Further, according to Francine the main goal of the afterlife is continued development of the soul and who better to learn from. She is not alone in this way of thinking. Whether you believe that Jesus is the Son of God, a major prophet, or a prominent rabbi and healer, the fact is he is a role model for all mankind. If only the power of love and forgiveness could be realized worldwide. I first came to believe in Jesus when I was meditating and focused on his life. Jesus was severely scourged, nailed to a cross, and left to bleed to death. Given all this he still asked his father: *"Forgive them for they know not what they do."* I can't imagine a normal man not being so filled with anger and fear that he hated his enemies and wished he could destroy them. Jesus of Nazareth was obviously not an ordinary man.

At this point in time I am so excited by the new findings and the implications for reversing the decline of society's moral decay that I have spoken to countless people about them. My shock was to find out that almost none were even aware of the military remote viewing program. If we are going to bring about change we need to better get the word out. Following my stroke, as I sat on the floor unable to speak or stand, my life flashed before my eyes. Over the next several weeks I meditated on this, and realized that several times I had been saved from dying. It was no accident that I became obsessed with learning everything I could about quantum physics. I believe I have a mission to perform, and that mission is to teach people that science supports belief in a creator and religion instills values and morals that bind mankind. Materialism and hedonism only tear us apart. I want to encourage everyone reading this to spread the word. The new paradigm of science has within it the potential to bring about change that the world desperately needs. We are all one. Everyone and everything is created from energy and all energy is entangled. While their will always be some ignorant people who remain bigoted against a whole class of people I do see change starting. We are all the children of our creator, and there is a deeper purpose for this life than materialistic hedonism. No one likes people who hurt others but to be bigoted against a whole group because of something like religion, skin color, sexual orientation or the size of ones nose is insane.

If we are going to survive as a species we must learn to overcome our differences and embrace our oneness. This is the message from the new paradigm of science. When minds are focused together we have the ability to effect change. The worldwide studies with random number generators have proven this. I remember reading in one of the new star wars books how the students and teachers from the Jedi academy focused their minds on throwing an armada of empire spaceships away from the moon they were settled on. It worked and the danger was averted.

Imagine if a billion or so people could all focus their minds on altering the course of an asteroid approaching collision with the earth. The new paradigm of science tells us that this is a possibility. The studies on prayer support this. Everything is entangled. Since governments are not preparing for the eventuality let's hope it works. As a race we are at the frontier of incredible change. We are evolving from a materialistic society to one that is coming to recognize the power of the human mind. In some ways we are finally recognizing the insights of our ancestors.

The question is will we be able to make the needed change before mankind destroys itself. In addition to the issues I have already discussed there is a major problem the world is facing. That problem is overpopulation. The world population continues to grow geometrically, and is the direct cause of depleting the oceans of fish, and of polluting the atmosphere and rivers. Further, overpopulation will lead to countries going to war over scarce natural resources. Fresh water is already becoming a major source of disputes. My own personal fear is that overpopulation is going to lead to mass malnutrition, deaths and diseases. Diseases are evolving to become deadlier and harder to treat as resistance to antibiotics increases. We now stand on a precipice. Will we come together and eventually become what physicist Michio Kaku calls a type 1 civilization or are we destined to continue on our destructive path and end the reign of man as a type 0 civilization? While it is not the exact meaning Dr. Kaku intended, to me a type 0 civilization is one that neglects its responsibility to be stewards of our planet. A type 1 civilization is one that has come to realize the oneness of all humanity and began to work together to solve common problems. Dinosaurs ruled the earth for more than a hundred million years. The question is will mankind make it for forty thousand years.

The next two hundred years should decide our fate.

I thank you for reading this book. If I have done my job well then I have opened your eyes to the fact that the new paradigm of science supports the immortality of consciousness, prayer helping to heal, and I personally believe the immortality of the soul as well. Further, it makes us realize that this life and this universe are not meaningless as Nobel Laureate physicist Steven Weinberg long believed but rather have a deeper purpose.

I would like to conclude this book with a prayer. Dear Lord: Grant us the wisdom to see the error of our ways. Help us to open our minds and hearts and come to accept the oneness of all people and all things. Help us to see that love for our fellow man is the key to ending the divisiveness that has beset man through the ages and is now threatening to end the reign of man on this planet.

APPENDIX 1

Treatment of Disabled Patients

Since working with individuals suffering emotional problems secondary to disabling physical injuries became such a big part of my practice for over twenty years I have experience and information that can be useful to any psychologist or mental health worker wishing to enter this practice specialty.

First of all remember the main issue on patient's minds is how will I support my family? This means that you will have to learn every option for securing their future income, and then do the required work to obtain it for them.

1. Workers Compensation Income
2. Social Security Disability Income
3. Short and Long-Term Disability Incomes
4. Disability Pensions
5. Medicare Savings plan (for low income)
6. Third Party Lawsuits

While these are the main sources of income you have to help them receive there are other options available to help patients financially.

Over time, and depending on the state you are in programs may change.

Next, remember to always consult with the referring physician and other doctors treating the patient. You want information that will help you better understand the disability and help with planning. Having the information will also better prepare you for testifying in court. Regarding court testifying, in the first fifteen years of my involvement with the Workers Compensation Board I would have to attend a trial once the IME psychiatrist rejected payment. Due to the difficulty in getting medical doctors to take time off from their practices to testify, in recent times depositions are taken over the phone. Some of your patients will also have third party lawsuits, and as the treating psychologist, you will occasionally have to testify in Supreme Court. Make sure you take careful notes, and get those medical reports in your file, because the defense attorney will carefully go through them to spot anything that can help his case. For example, you're giving one diagnosis and then making a different diagnosis shortly thereafter. There may be a reason for this, but they will question you on it. I remember the first time I had to testify in Supreme Court. My hands were literally shaking. By the second time I had realized the strategy of the defense lawyer was to question your credibility, and was prepared for him. My hands only shook a little. One example will make the point to be prepared for attacks. The defense lawyer took my case file and looked through the notes. While looking at the jury he said " *Dr. Alne you call yourself a professional. Look at these notes. Your handwriting is terrible. A child could do better.*" I calmly responded " *I apologize for the handwriting but the fact is I would much rather interact with my patient and help him instead of being overly concerned with writing notes for others.*"

Remember also that when a person becomes totally disabled it is the whole family that is impacted. I routinely ask to see the spouse to involve them in the process, and also to let them know that I am aware of their pain. Children also may need to be seen.

If you are going to develop this as a specialty it is extremely helpful to receive training in pharmacology and related medical science. Fortunately there are more and more continuing education programs out there. Not only is this helpful for your patients since you will be the one seeing them most often and monitoring their condition, but medical doctors will come to see you in a different light and become referral sources. On a few occasions I was able to identify prescribed medications that could cause dangerous interactions and notified the physicians. On other occasions I noted side effects that needed to be addressed. Treating disabled patients truly requires you to "treat the whole person." Over time, and with training and experience, you will also be able to counter any questionable advice patients have been given.

Be aware there are medical doctors out there who care more for their pockets than they do for the welfare of the patient. You are their advocate. Here I have the perfect example. A physiatrist (Doctor of Rehabilitation Medicine) had referred a workers' compensation patient to me for psychotherapy. One day he called and asked if I would come meet with him in his office. As I got to his office I noticed that the shades were drawn so that it was impossible to see inside. As I entered the office I noticed six small cubicles on the left side. Each contained a treatment table and a stepper. In the last cubicle was an oriental woman who looked like a bag lady. A patient told me she was an acupuncturist. The Russian doctor didn't even say hello. He blurted out *"I want you to come work for me."* I thanked him, but mentioned that I had a very busy private practice and so was unable to. His next words were *"You no work for me then leave."* I am sure he was very helpful to patients.

As a treating therapist you must be an advocate for your patients. Help them avoid such obvious scams, and believe me they are out there.

The main point I worked to achieve in almost all patients is that "You are injured but not dead." I did everything I could to help them develop a new career or interest to make them feel positive about themselves. Some patients I treated developed or participate in websites. Others have opened their own businesses once a case settled and, while not performing physical labor, managed them. Many patients became volunteers, and one developed the most unusual interest of all. This person got involved in the porn trade. He traveled to the yearly convention of the industry. That year it happened to be on the West Coast. There he met the two largest porn producers. He overheard them speaking Yiddish, and he began speaking Yiddish to them. He found himself with a job opportunity. It appears that the girls make most of their money by making appearances at clubs. My patient made all arrangements for their visits to New York, and picked them up in a limousine. I can only imagine what his wife thought. My wife would have killed me. Eventually she did make him stop.

The goal of the therapist is to make the disabled individual feel worthwhile and involved in life. Accomplish this and you have saved a life. One thing I know to be a fact is that working with disabled individuals, and helping them cope with their pain and fears, helped me deal with my own pain and fears, and also educated me regarding effective treatments.

Before I leave this issue there is one warning I need to give to people who find themselves with disabilities. Lawyers today are asking patients, when they first meet, to sign for them to represent the person when applying for Social Security Disability. <u>Do Not Let Them Do This</u>. When applying for Social Security Disability tell patients to first make their doctors aware of their intentions. If they are on board the patient will then fill out the application online. Next the patient should keep in touch with the social security examiner to make sure that he or she receives all necessary reports from the doctors. From my experience, sometimes reports are lost in the mailroom or misfiled. Should the Social Security Board require additional medical information it will send the patient to its doctors, and, unlike workers compensation IME doctors, its doctors do not have financial incentive to lie. Lawyers are to be used only if a patient is turned down, and they wish to appeal their case. The five thousand dollar fee they are awarded is better in the patient's pocket.

REFERENCES

Alexander, Eben. 2012. *Proof of Heaven: A Neurosurgeons Journey into the Afterlife.* New York: Simon and Schuster.

Andrews, Synthia and Andrews, Colin. 2010. *The Complete Idiot's Guide to The Akashic Records.* Orlando, Florida : Alpha Press.

Astsor, Herman. 2010. *The Cave and the Light: Plato versus Aristotle and the Struggle for the Soul of Western Civilization.* New York: Random House.

Behe, Michael, J. 2007. *The Edge of Evolution: The Search for the Limits of Darwinism.* New York: Free Press.

Bell, John. 1993. *Speakable and Unspeakable in Quantum Mechanics.* Cambridge, England: University Press.

Benor, Daniel. 2000. *Spiritual Healing: Scientific Validation of A Healing Revolution.* Lancashire, England: Vision Publications.

Bohm, David. 2002. *Wholeness and the Implicate Order.* London, England: Routledge Classics.

Browne, Sylvia. 2005. *Contacting Your Spirit Guide. New York: Hay House*

Capra, Fritjof. 2010. *The Tao of Physics: An Exhortation of the Parallels Between Modern Physics and Eastern Mysticism.* Berkeley, California: Shambhala Press.

Doidge, Norman. 2007. *The Brain That Changes Itself: Stories of Personal Triumphs from the Frontiers of Brain Science.* New York: Penguin Books.

Dawkins, Richard. 2008. *The God Delusion.* New York: Mariner Books.

Daniel, Matt. 2006. *The Essential Kabbalah: The Heart of Jewish Mysticism.* New York: HarperOne.

Dossey, Larry. 1999. *Reinventing Medicine: Beyond Mind-Body to a New Era of Medicine.* Califonia: HarperSanFransisco.

Dossey, Larry. 2009. *The Power of Premonitions: How Knowing the future Can Shape Our Lives.* New York: Dutton.

Edwards, John. 1999. *One Last Time: A Psychic Medium Speaks to Those we have Loved and Lost.* New York: Signet.

Ellis Albert. 2004. *Rational Emotive Behavior Therapy: It Works for me-It can Work for you.* New York: Prometheus Books.

Ent, Rolf, Ullrich, Thomas and Venugopalon, Rajo. "How Do Gluons Bind Matter" Scientific American, May 2015, pages 42-49.

Ferguson, Kitty. 2002. *Tycho and Kepler.* London, England: Walker Books.

Feynman, Richard and Leighton, Ralph. 1997. *Surely You're Joking Mr. Feynman.* New York: W.W. Norton and Co.

Fox, R.E., DeLeon, P.H., Newman, R., Sammons, M.T., Dunivin, D.L., Baeker, D.C. 2009. "Prescriptive Authority and Psychology: A Status Era of Healing Report." American Psychologist, 64 (4) 257-268.

•Ford, Kenneth & Wheeler, John, Archibald. 1998. *Geons, Black Holes and Quantum Foam: A Life in Physics.* New York, W.W. Norton.

Gefter, Amanda. 2014. *Tresspassing on Einstein's Lawn. A Father, a Daughter, the Meaning of Nothing, and the Beginning of Everything.* New York: Bantom.

Glashow, Sheldon and Bova, Ben. 1988. *Interactions: A Journey Through the Mind of a Particle Physicist and the Matter of This World.* New York: Warner Books.

Gribbin, J. 2009. *In Search of the Multiverse.* Hoboken, New Jersey: John Wiley & Sons Inc.

Greenstein, George. 1988. *Symbiotic Universe: Life And Mind In The Cosmos.* New York: William Morrow and Co.

Greene, Brian: 2011. *The Hidden Reality: Parallel Universes And The Deep Laws Of The Cosmos.* New York: Alfred A. Knopf.

Goswami, Amit, Goswami, M. and Reed, Richard E. 1995. *The Self-Aware Universe: How consciousness creates the material world.* New York: Penguin Putnam.

Grayson, Henry. 2012. *Use Your Body To Heal Your Mind: Revolutionary Methods to Release all Barriers to Health, Healing and Happiness.* New York: Balboa Press.

Hagerty, Barbara. 2009. *Fingerprints of God: The Search For the Science of Spirituality. New York: Riverhead Books.*

Hamilton, Allan. 2009. *The Soul and The Scalpel: Encounters With Surgery, The Supernatural and the Healing Power of Hope.* New York: TarcherPerigee

Hoyle, Fred. 1988. *The Intelligent Universe.* New York: Holt, Rinehart & Winton.

Hubble, Edwin & Bartusiak, Marcia. 2010. *The Day we Found the Universe.* New York: Vintage Books.

Kaku, Michio. 2011. *Physics Of The Future: How Science Will Shape Human Destiny And Our Daily Lives By The Year 2100.* New York: Anchor Books.

Kelly, Robin. 2011. *The Human Hologram: Living Your Life in Harmony with the Unified Field.* Santa Rosa, California: Energy Psychology Press.

Kirkpatrick, Sidney D. 2000. *Edgar Cayce: An American Prophet.* New York: Riverhead Books.

Krauss, Lawrence. 1989. *The Fifth Essence: The Search For Dark Matter in The Universe.* New York: Basic Books.

Lanza, Robert & Berman, Bob. 2009. *Biocentrism.* Dallas, Texas: BenBella.

Leary, Timothy. 1999. *Turn on, Tune in, Drop out.* Berkeley, California: Ronin Publishing.

Manjit, Kumar. 2011. *Quantum: Einstein, Bohr and the Great Debate About the Nature of Reality.* New York: W.W. Norton.

Mann, Charles, C. 2011. *The Birth of Religion: The World's First Temple.* National Geographic Magazine, June 2011, 34-59.

McNamara, Parrick, 2006. *Where God and Science Meet: How Brain and Evolutionary Studies Alter our Understanding of Religion.* Westport, Conneticut: Praeger.

Margolis, Jonathan. 1999. *Uri Geller: Magician or Mystic.* New York: Welcome Rain Publishers.

McCormick, Anita, Louise. 1998. *The Industrial Revolution in American History.* New Jersey: Enslow.

Mehl-Madrona, Lewis. 1998. *Coyote Medicine: Lessons from Native American Healing.* New York: Simon and Schuster.

Monroe, Robert A. 1992. *Journey's Out of The Body.* New York: Broadway Books.

Monroe, Robert A. 1996. Ultimate Journey. Goshen, KY: Harmony Publishers.

Morehouse, David. 1998. *Psychic Warrior: The True Story of America's Foremost Psychic Spy and the Cover-Up of the CIA'S Top-Secret Stargate Program.* New York: St. Martin's Press.

Morowitz, Harold. 1979. *Energy Flow and Biology.* Oxford, England: OxBow Press.

Morse, Melvin. 2001. *Where God Lives: The Science of The Paranormal and How Our Brains are Linked to The Universe.* New York: HarperOne.

Neal, Mary. 2012. *To Heaven and Back: A Doctor's Extraordinary Account of Her Death, Heaven, Angels and Life Again: A True Story.* Colorado Springs, Colorado. Water Brook Press.

Penrose, Roger, Hameroff, Stuart, Stapp, Henry and Chopra, Deepak. 2011. *Consciousness and The Universe: Quantum Physics, Evolution, Brain and Mind.* New York: Cosmology Science Publishers.

Piaget, Jean. 2001. *The Psychology of Intelligence.* London, England: Routledge Classics.

Radin, Dean. 2006. *Entangled Minds: Extrasensory Experiences in a Quantum Reality.* New York: Paraview Books.

Radin, Dean. 1997. *The Conscious Universe: The Scientific Truth of Psychic Phenomena.* New York: HarperOne.

Robock, Alan & Toon, Brian. *South Asian Threat: Nuclear War= Global Suffering.* Scientific American, June, 2010, 62-69.

Rosenblum, Bruce & Kuttner, Fred. 2011. *Quantum Enigma: Physics Encounters Consciousness.* New York: Oxford University Press.

Sabom, Michael: 1998. *Light and Death.* New York: Zondervan.

Schroeder, Gerald. 1997. *The Science of God: The Convergence of Scientific and Biblical Wisdom.* New York: Broadway Books.

Schroeder, Gerald. 1991. *Genesis and the Big Bang: The Discovery of Harmony Between Science and The Bible.* New York: Bantom Books.

Schwartz, Gary & Russek, Linda. 2003. *The Afterlife Experiments: Breakthrough Scientific Evidence of Life After Death.* New York: Atria Books.

Sheldrake, Rupert. 1995. *Morphic Resonance: The Nature of Formative Causation.* Vermont: Park Street Press.

Shapiro, Edward, S. 2006. *Crown Heights: Blacks and Jews and The 1991 Brooklyn Riots.* New York: Brandeis.

Smith, Paul. 2005. *Reading the Enemy's Mind: Inside Stargate America's Psychic Espionage Program.* New York: MacMillan.

Smolin, Lee. 2014. *Time Reborn: From the Crisis in Physics to the Future of the Universe.* New York: Mariner Books.

Stager, Curt. 2014. *Your Atomic Self. The Invisible Elements That Connect You to Everything in the Universe.* New York: St. Martin's Press.

Talbot, Michael. 1988. *Beyond The Quantum: How the Secrets of the New Physics are Bridging the Chasm Between Science and Faith.* New York: Bantom Books.

Targ, Russell. 2004. *Limitless Mind: A Guide to Remote Viewing and Transformation of Consciousness.* Novato, California: New World Library.

Tompkins, Peter, and Bird, Christopher. 1989. *The Secret Life of Plants: A Fascinating Account of the Physical, Emotional and Spiritual Relations Between Plants and Man.* New York: Harper and Row.

VanPragh, James. 1999. *Talking to Heaven: A Mediums Message of Life After Death.* New York: Signet.

Weinberg, Steven. 1977. *The First Three Minutes: A Modern View of the Universe.* New York, Basic Books.

Wheeler, John & Wingate, Stephen. 2008. *The Light Behind Consciousness.* New York: Non-Duality Press.

Zukav, Gary. 2009. *The Dancing Wuli Masters.* New York: HarperOne

Printed in the United States
By Bookmasters